# Hidden Teachings of the Mystic I-Ching:
## Activating the Gateways to the Many Lives of the Spectral Soul

*American Tao Series, Book Two*

S.Strasnick, PhD

Mystic Tao
Publishing

ISBN-13: 978-0-9976471-1-2
ISBN-10: 0-9976471-1-6

Cover Art, Book Design & Graphics:
Steven Strasnick

Special thanks to my wife Katie, without whom none of this book could have been written

Printed in the United States of America

Mystic Tao Publishing
stevos2000@icloud.com
Santa Cruz, CA

# Hidden Teachings of the Mystic I-Ching:
## Activating the Gateways to the Many Lives of the Spectral Soul

Including the Author's Visionary Travels to Other Worlds

*An American Tao Book*

The *American Tao* books, of which *Hidden Teachings of the Mystic I-Ching* is the second, are unlike anything you will ever read. They present the true story of what happened when a skeptical, spiritual neophyte sat down to begin a daily practice of meditation and somehow slid through a crack between worlds, ultimately ending up in a strange new psychic dimension of the Multi-Soul. Unbeknownst to him, he had been called. He had become the accidental mystic, a traveller of worlds.

In repeated visits over an extended period, the author experienced over seventy strange visions and apparitions. These led him on a journey across multiple realms and worlds, ultimately taking him into the celestial chambers of a mysterious white-bearded being, where final secrets were revealed. This book presents new theories about the hidden mystical teachings of the I-Ching and the true nature of the soul, along with a description of sixty-four of the author's visionary travels to other worlds.

# About the Author, In His Own Words

## The Story of an Errant Seeker

When I began this endeavor I was not a mystic. In many ways, I was as far from a mystic as you could get. My soul was calling to me, but I couldn't hear its message beneath the frantic hubbub of my life. Only the quiet stillness of meditation allowed me to hear its voice.

Over the years, I earned degrees from world-class universities, including a BS from MIT, a PhD in philosophy from Harvard and an MBA from UC Berkeley. My professional life reflected this diverse background. I worked as a philosophy professor at Stanford University, a programmer manager at IBM and SGI, a programmer and digital artist at media and education start-ups, a researcher in space biology at NASA Ames, and a bioinformatics engineer at Silicon Genetics and Agilent Technology.

Reflecting on my life, I wondered what unknown forces might have been driving me. But then, serendipitously, I stumbled on a method that opened doors to the hidden realms of the mystic world, pulling me in. All my varied accomplishments turned out to be so much smoke and mirrors. My background may not have prepared me for the journey I was to undertake, but it did help me tell the tale of what I encountered along the way and the truths that the journey would reveal.

# Some Words of Insight

Alice laughed: "There's no use trying," she said; "one can't believe impossible things." "I daresay you haven't had much practice," said the Queen. "When I was younger, I always did it for half an hour a day. Why, sometimes I've believed as many as six impossible things before breakfast."
--- Lewis Caroll, aka Charles Lutwidge Dogson,
in *Through the Looking Glass and What Alice Found There*

"In my Father's house are many mansions: if *it were not so*, I would have told you. I go to prepare a place for you."
-- Jesus, *King James Bible*, John 14:2

"If you bring forth what is within you, what you have will save you. If you do not have that within you,
what you do not have within you will kill you."
-- Jesus, *The Gospel of Thomas* (70)

"One who is whole will be filled with light,
but one who is fragmented will be filled with darkness."
-- Jesus, *The Gospel of Thomas* (61)

"When you make the two into one, when you make
the inner like the outer and the outer like the inner,
and the upper like the lower,
when you make the male and female into a single one,
so that the male will not be male,
and the female will not be female,
when you make eyes replacing an eye, ...,
and an image replacing an image,
then you will enter the kingdom."
-- Jesus, *The Gospel of Thomas* (22)

# Table of Contents

About the Author, In His Own Words ........................ ii
Some Words of Insight ............................ v
Preface to the *American Tao* Series: ...................... viii
The Theory of the Spectral Soul .......................... 1
    What Meditation Has Wrought ........................ 2
    The Six Impossible Things ........................ 3
    The Theory of the Soul .......................... 4
    The Spectral Soul ........................ 4
    Visions and the Etheric Body ..................... 12

The I-Ching and the Spectral Soul ...................... 17
    The I Ching ..................... 18
    Yin and Yang ..................... 18
    Trigrams and the Ba Gua ..................... 21
    The Hexagrams (Gua) ..................... 25
    Hexagram Scoring Criteria ..................... 28
    Transformations on Hexagrams (Gua) ..................... 33
    The Hub Activation Process ..................... 34

I Ching Trigram Interpretation ........................... 40
    The Soul's Transformative Journey ..................... 41
    The Five Phases ..................... 42
    Associations with Trigram Levels ..................... 45

The Eight Trigrams ..................... 48
A New Approach to the I-Ching ..................... 57
    The Traditional I-Ching ..................... 58
    The Visionary I-Ching ..................... 59
    Major Subjects and Personas within the Visions ..... 63

The Visionary I-Ching: 64 Gua & Visions ................. 65
Appendixes ..................... 194
    Appendix A: Trigram and Gua Lookup Table .......... 195
    Appendix B: Trigram Hexagram Power Score ......... 196
    Appendix B: Gua Gateway Scores per Level ......... 196
    Appendix C: Gateway Activation Sites per Level.... 197
    Appendix D: Gua with Power and Dual Scores........ 198

Appendix E: Gua with Associated Visions.............. 200
Appendix F: Gua with Trigram Interpretation ....... 202
Appendix G: Gua Power Scores......................... 204
Appendix H: Inner Root Gua and Cycles .............. 205
Appendix I: The Inner Root Cycles .................... 206
Appendix J: Gua and Inner Root Dual Score ......... 208
Appendix K: Gua and Root Dual Score Ranking ....... 210
Appendix L: References................................ 212

Coming Next ........................................... 213

# Preface to the *American Tao* Series:
## Books One and Two

On December 27th, 2014 I sat down to begin what I hoped would become a daily practice of meditation, not suspecting that my world was about to irrevocably change. Within minutes of closing my eyes I witnessed the first of many strange visions and apparitions that would visit me over the next year and a half, the vast majority occurring within the first three months before starting to diminish in frequency. I had somehow opened the floodgates to the worlds of my unconscious.

At first, surprisingly, I did not consider these experiences unusual or deserving of further study. Like you, I've learned to accept my nighttime dreams as a normal part of life. These just seemed a kind of daytime dream. If anything, I found them entertaining. I simply assumed that they, like dreams, were something that happened when you slipped into an alternative state of consciousness, something best experienced and then quickly forgotten. After all, that was the advice offered by all the introductory books on meditation I looked at.

Over the next couple of months, as these experiences continued to accumulate, my perspective started to change. My curiosity began to grow. Was what was happening to me typical? I talked to many long-term meditators and asked them about their experiences. I dove into the mystical literature to see if I could discover historical antecedents to my experiences. While none of the people I talked to reported anything remotely similar, I did find examples in history of mystics who had.

Things grew even stranger for me on March 24th, 2015. On that day approximately 45 minutes into my meditation session, I experienced what I subsequently refer to in this book as "The Incursion." Several things occurred simultaneously. It began with my awareness suddenly snapping back into the ordinary world from whatever kind of trance state I had been in. The first thing I noticed was that the CD player in my room that had been playing soft meditation music was now skipping wildly, like the old fashioned phonograph, repeatedly jumping back to the same spot, in an endless loop. The volume seemed much louder as well. I thought the room was shaking. My body definitely was.

As more physical sensations returned to me, I realized that I had been hyperventilating, breathing dramatically quicker than I normally did during meditation. More significantly, I felt a torrent of energy streaming into the top of my head and down my spine, where it seemed to settle in my lower abdominal region, below my navel. I did not experience this energy as painful, though it was certainly intense. Words don't really suffice, but the best way to describe it was to call it a physical experience of ecstatic bliss.

In my readings I had learned about the phenomenon of the Kundalini experience, in which energy reportedly shot up the practitioner's spine. This seemed like a variant of that experience, a kind of reverse Kundalini. The physical aftershocks from this experience reverberated through my meditation sessions for the next week. The psychic aftershocks, which carried over into my everyday life, lasted much longer.

Since that event, I have often calmed myself with the thought that I knew "why the Buddha smiled." At times I considered that this phrase would make a good title for the account I soon felt compelled to write. Because of that event and others that followed it, I finally accepted both the uniqueness and the strangeness of what was happening to me. The rationalist in me felt the accumulated body of all these experiences deserved further study and documentation. The books of the *American Tao* series are the result.

The first book in the series, *Meditation's Secret Treasure* (MST), begins the story (Strasnick, 2016). While the tale it tells focuses on the process of my mystical awakening, the nature of my experiences are not unique to me but have been encountered by many others who have walked a similar path. Because of this it can be read as a kind of travel log, one that paves the way for your own travels. Among the topics it covers are: the kinds of initiation events that signal the beginning of a major shift in consciousness, how visions test and prepare the practitioner for travels to different worlds, and how childhood events can summon you onto the mystic path.

For those who are ready to begin their own journeys, MST provides all the information needed to start a meditative practice. It not only presents a simple and proven method for meditation, but also includes the philosophical grounding for this practice in the mystical teachings of Taoism. Once experiences begin, it shows how to record and analyze them in order to gain a deeper understanding. And, of course, it includes descriptions and commentary for my first nine visions and the four iconic dreams from earlier in my life that first opened the doors to the mystic worlds.

This second book, *Hidden Teachings of the Mystic I-Ching*, is different in kind and in some ways more ambitious. While it does include a description of the remaining set of all my visions, sixty-four in total, both those in which I travelled to other worlds as well as those where forces and apparitions from those other worlds travelled here, that is not its primary focus. Its main purpose is to present what those visions taught me.

Based upon what I learned from them, I have formulated a new philosophical theory about the nature of the self and the role visions play in its discovery and liberation. This self is expressed through what I call the spectral soul, a being whose journey takes it far beyond its current incarnation in a process of evolution that spans many lives and lifetimes.

A key part of that evolution occurs during this life, for the soul must reach out to other of its lives in order to evolve; it does this in search of the liberation that someday will be found in an act of transcendent unification where its consciousness expands into an awareness that simultaneously extends across many lifetimes.

A major impetus for this theory was triggered by my discovery of an entirely new layer of meaning hidden in an ancient Chinese classic, the I-Ching. Following a series of clues from within my visions, I found a new way of looking at the symbolic pictograms of the I-Ching that directly illuminated the nature of the process by which the spectral soul evolved. This discovery was further supported by a series of direct experiences that I had during meditation of the forces of the human energy field, known as the etheric body.

Rather than reading the I-Ching in the traditional manner as a manual for divination, I came to understand the sixty-four symbols of the I-Ching as representing the different energetic configurations of our etheric body, in particular, ones involved in opening the gateways to other worlds and lives. Perhaps my most important discovery was that the visions that arose during meditation provided the very vehicle for the soul's evolution and ultimate liberation.

I begin this book by mapping out the major elements of my theory of the spectral soul, which I develop in a series of numbered propositions, leading to a new approach for I-Ching analysis and scoring. With this foundation I present an enhanced formulation of the sixty-four pictogram chapters making up the main body of the I-Ching.

I will illustrate the meaning of each chapter with one of my sixty-four visions rather than with the traditional Chinese folktales from thousands of years ago. The account of the I-Ching that results is a structured, mystic re-visioning of the original work and can be studied along with more traditional accounts to attain a deeper understanding of the nature of the soul's process of change and transformation.

While this book utilizes the traditional I-Ching order in its presentation of my visions, the third volume of the *American Tao* series will focus on the original narrative order in which the visions were received. The resulting I-Ching sequence will be the one experienced by the monadic-soul during its visionary travelling. This next book, tentatively titled *Many Lives, Many Worlds*, will use the methodology developed here to plot the progress of gateway and channel activation within the etheric body receiving the visions. This progress will be measured by tracking the energetic contributions of the gua that represent each vision.

# The Theory of the Spectral Soul

*"The world is a song,*
*and we are its colors."*
*--Anonymous*

(Actually, this came to me uninvited, while
on a walk through a grassy meadow,
before I had even thought about
starting to meditate.)

## What Meditation Has Wrought

Most of us spend our lives secure in the beliefs that this embodied life is the only one we get, that the world we experience within wakened consciousness is the real one and the only one that exists, that we live, in other words, one life in one world. I say "us" because I too had these beliefs.

But then everything changed, not all at once, but rather, turning Hemingway's often-misquoted passage on its head, "Suddenly, then gradually." During an initially intense period lasting three months, and then more slowly over a year and a half, I witnessed a series of extraordinary visionary events, primarily during meditation, that fundamentally overturned my most basic beliefs about life and the world.

I don't make this claim casually, since I have been trained both as a scientist and a philosopher, but I have come to trust the reporting of both my outer and inner senses. Confronted with the full spectrum of all that I experienced, I tried to adopt a more scientific attitude, intending to follow the dictum: "observe and analyze." That is what I have done, in an exercise of what might be called speculative philosophy, while writing this book and other volumes of the *American Tao* series.

As a result of my experiences, long-held beliefs about the nature of reality and the self have been replaced by a new set of convictions. I can summarize these in the form of six main thoughts, which, following Lewis Caroll, I call the "Six Impossible Things." Together, these constitute the key elements of a new theory about the meaning of life and the nature of the soul, one in which the number six will come to play a significant role.

Even though I say "new," much of what I believe echoes the teachings of the great masters who have had their own mystical journeys, though in other places and times. But my visions have provided me with a somewhat different slant on how all the pieces fit together, resulting in a new kind of synthesis.

## The Six Impossible Things

These, in outline form, are the elements of the message I believe my soul, through my meditational visions, was trying to communicate to me. Ascribing intent to visions might seem like an odd position to take, but it rests on the core principle that if the purpose of visions is to guide us towards enlightenment, then the visions will contain within them the clues to their own illumination. The "you" being addressed here is I.

(1) "You are not your material body and you will not die. But experiences of other lifetimes will only be available to you if your consciousness is open to experiences that are normally suppressed."

(2) "Neither are you the autonomous and unitary self you thought you were. It is not just that you are subject to the diverse biological, material, and cultural forces that shape all your needs and desires. More importantly, you are, in your deepest nature, a manifold of other beings simultaneously alive in other places and times."

(3) "The world in which you spend your waking life is only one of many, existing on parallel planes of being just beyond your own, beginning with the one 'right next door.'"

(4) "Reincarnation is real, but not in the way you think. Your 'next' life is not always in your historical future, nor even in the same timeline or on the same world."

(5) "Each life is a step on your evolutionary journey. In order to progress on this path and not stagnate, you have to expand your consciousness by creating psychic connections to your other lives while in this one."

(6) "Your psychic connections to these other lives are established through the energetic channels and gateways of your etheric body, which need to be activated in order to establish more substantial connections."

## The Theory of the Soul

Taken together, these statements, whose truth once seemed impossible to me, are part of a larger, more encompassing theory of the soul, which I call the *Theory of the Spectral Soul*:

> You are a spark of the divine spirit, which has been embodied within a tomb of living matter and dispersed as soul among your many lives. Your task, over the course of these lives, is to nurture this spark and repair this fragmentation by reintegrating these many lives into a new whole. Only then will you be able to free your true self from the dark confines of matter, to emerge into the full light of wakened consciousness, free to live as creator instead of in bondage to the created.

This statement of the theory should sound very familiar to students of the mystic tradition, since, as part of the so-called perennial philosophy, it has appeared before in many other forms and guises. The differences between these other traditions and the message of this work will emerge in the new kind of synthesis it seeks between their disparate teachings. I present this synthesis aphoristically in the following sections, as notes transcribed from my journals, once again in the form of communications from my soul to my self.

.

## The Spectral Soul

Aspects of my visionary experiences heavily influenced my belief in the following statements about the existence of parallel lives and the soul's evolutionary drive: both from what I took to be the symbolic content of many of my visions and the fact that I so often assumed the direct identity of the experiencing subject while within the vision.

The additional fact that these identities and their associated story lines often persisted across separate meditation sessions seemed important to me. It suggested that these narratives had an independent existence that continued to unfold outside of my direct experience of them, creating gaps in my ability to understand the full chronologies of their events.

Note 0. You, like everything else in existence, contain within you something of the divine, though the amount possessed will vary greatly. The possibility of experiencing anything of the divine should make you want to have more. There is a way. The fact that you are here now means that someday you will have succeeded beyond your wildest dreams. But to get there you still had to make the journey.

Note 1. It is important not to get ahead of your self. You are not God, nor are you divine in any meaningful way. Not yet, anyways. The miniscule, flickering spark of the divine spirit that you contain no more makes you God than being a drop of water makes you the ocean. Were it otherwise, you would know.

Note 2. The divine spirit that is within you has been buried so deeply within the pit of nature's dark matter as to be barely visible or accessible except within the quietest depths of meditation or in the deepest sleep. To quote the title of a book by Scott Adams, the creator of *Dilbert*, you are, in his words, "God's Debris." But if you had to be made of something, wouldn't you want it to be God-stuff?

Note 3. In spite of this fact, even the smallest spark of the divine spirit is infinitely more powerful than the blind matter in which it is entombed. Since divine spirit is by nature aware of its destiny and calling, it will always attempt in each life to propel itself forward along its evolutionary path.

Note 4. Your willingness to open yourself in your life to hearing your spirit's message is a measure of the progress you have made and have yet to make. To be open to this message you must accept your own smallness and insignificance in the light of what you might someday become. You must surrender yourself to your spirit's calling.

Note 5. The light from this divine spark, besides being the immanent force that gives life to inanimate matter and creates all consciousness and self-awareness, is also the source behind the creation of the soul.

Note 6. Your soul is not a separately existing being. Rather, it is the spiritual shadow cast by the light of the divine spirit shining through the material matrix of your physical embodiment. The luminescence of your soul-spirit and the depth of your consciousness will increase in proportion to the degree of growth and integration of your divine spirit.

Note 7. The soul-spirit, as a manifestation of divine spirit, is an undifferentiated unity, in its essence unblemished, shining with a pure light. However, just as a pure white light is decomposed into a series of colored bands when passed through a prismatic lens, so too is the pure soul fragmented into a series of separate spirits when embodied and observed through the distorting eyes of material being.

Note 8. Your many lives reveal the fragmented nature of the spectral soul, dispersed through space and time in the realm of the Multi-Soul. While the pure soul-spirit is a wavelike undifferentiated entity, until it is reintegrated, it will be experienced discretely through the consciousness of multiple lives spread across multiple parallel worlds.

Note 9. The vast majority of these lives will possess only a dreaming soul prior to their achieving waking consciousness within the scope of a mundane world. The enormity of the universe is so great that from your fragmented perspective, the number of souls in the spiritual network is infinitely large.

Note 10. Even though the soul-spirit has been dispersed across an essentially infinite number of multiple lifelines, each incarnation within a mundane world will tend to view its life and soul as the only one. Prior to a larger enlightenment, you will experience your life only through the witnessing consciousness of your waking-soul, which is expressed in the form of both your external personality and your ego.

Note 11. Since the soul-spirit is an evolving entity traveling along an evolutionary path, while in this fragmented state, only one life will truly embody the soul-spirit at a given stage of its evolution. That life, as a primary incarnation within a mundane world, will embody the primary or monadic-soul. For that life, because of the presence the monadic-soul, the dreaming-soul will achieve a higher level of awareness, becoming the waking-soul.

Note 12. The Multi-Soul is like a planetary system, in which living planets revolve around the sun, or like the atomic model, in which electrons occupy different energetic orbitals at increasing distances from the nucleus. The monadic-soul is the central nucleus or sun around which all the other lesser souls orbit and from which they derive their energy and sustenance. The waking-soul is the one closest to it.

Note 13. The monadic-soul is active within the incarnation that represents the highest developed form of the divine spirit along its evolutionary path, as present in the embodiment currently endowed with full waking consciousness. You view your lives through the eyes of your waking-soul, which having been roused from its dreaming life has now become more conscious -- within the limitations of the mundane world.

Note 14. Once the monadic-soul has completed its passage through a particular embodiment, that incarnation and its accompanying waking-soul and memories will fade from the Multi-Soul. Memories require a physical embodiment for their persistence and experience, and since the monadic-soul is a spiritual entity, the only memories available to it are those formed from its experiences while within its current physical embodiment.

Note 15. Only the lives and worlds still to be experienced by the monadic-soul remain in the Multi-Soul. The dreaming-souls that remain constitute the panorama of lives waiting to be traversed in the soul's evolutionary journey. As the monadic-soul evolves, the number of potential lifetimes available in the future will decrease. This number is so large, however, that it will essentially never be exhausted. From a temporal standpoint, new lives will continue to be generated in one or more of the multiple world timelines, which themselves are also constantly being renewed as the timelines of others expire.

Note 16. Within the timeless perspective of the pure soul-spirit, all these remaining potential lives and worlds have already been experienced within the consciousness of their dreaming-souls. To these dreaming-souls, their bodies and worlds seemed real, their lives filled with the same kinds of experiences, both good and bad, as ours. But for the pure soul-spirit, these deeds and destinies have already been written in the book of life. But they have not yet been experienced through the immanent consciousness of the monadic-soul.

Note 17. From the temporal perspective of the mundane world, these embodied dreaming-souls represent future lives, though not in the normal sense of the word. They are in the future only with respect to the monadic-soul's evolutionary journey. The soul isn't bound to the chronology of the physical world, though each world has a place in that chronology. For the evolving soul, a future life is one in which it has attained at least the same or higher level of development.

Note 18. As a result, even though your current monadic-soul's incarnation is embodied in the 21$^{st}$ century, your next one is just as likely to take you back in historical time as it is to jump you forward into some future reality. It may even put you back into the same one. Nothing about the level of cultural or technological development within a given historical epoch precludes the development of higher levels of spirituality by individuals within it. Within any particular time period, there will no doubt exist a wide spectrum of souls at various levels of development.

Note 19. Because the evolution of the monadic-soul is not bound by the constraints of historicity or a linear timeline, it is quite possible for multiple incarnations of the monadic-soul to be active within the same historical time period. This means not only that there might currently exist multiple incarnations of the same monadic-soul in the here and now, but also that these souls might come into contact or even regularly interact with one another. This was possible because these souls were currently at different levels in their spiritual development.

Note 20. The monadic-soul does not die, nor does it regress in its evolutionary development. At the death of its current physical embodiment, it will move into that next physical form and associated lifetime that will be able to successfully embody its monadic-soul at its current level of development. The experiences of that lifetime must be ones that will support the progress the monadic-soul has already achieved in its previous incarnation.

Note 21. Within the new incarnation, the presence of the monadic-soul will transform the formerly dreaming-soul into a waking one. That life will be essentially replayed, but through the witnessing eyes of the monadic-soul and newly conscious waking-soul. Due to the transformative power of the underlying soul-spirit, the presence of the monadic-soul in that life will have the capacity to dynamically alter key elements of that life, potentially rewriting its story in the book of life.

Note 22. The reason you are sometimes able to have glimpses of events in your lives that have yet to happen is due to the fact that your life is recurrent, one that has already occurred from the timeless perspective of the soul-spirit but is now being re-experienced by the monadic-soul as part of its evolutionary journey.

Note 23. Within the next life, the monadic-soul will no longer be directly in touch with memories from its previous life. However, if in a previous lifetime it had shared experiences with that future incarnation, that later incarnation will have formed new memories of the experience shared from the previous lifetime.

Note 24. The dreaming-souls and their associated lifelines exist in dimensions occurring simultaneously with that of the present historical incarnation of the monadic-soul. These different lifelines are not synchronized with the timeline of the current incarnation, nor are they occurring at the same pace.

Note 25. The monadic-soul can access these lives by establishing channels of communication between them. This capacity for inter-life experience is one that gradually evolves along with the other powers of the monadic-soul and is transferred from lifetime to lifetime. Like the soul's other powers, it needs to be strengthened and refined in each incarnation to further the soul's evolutionary progress. Future lives contain a treasure trove of potential new experiences for the soul in its current incarnation.

Note 26. As the communication channels between the present and future lifetimes become more robust, the monadic-soul will be able to view episodes from these other lifelines with increasing realism. It will be able to jump into specific points in these other lives to supplement the experiences of its present life. These experiences become the basis of new memories accessible to the monadic-soul during its current incarnation as well as providing the soul with potentially revelatory glimpses into the future course of its spiritual evolution.

Note 27. The monadic-soul will not only be able to monitor and experience events in those future lives but also share some of its current experiences with the future life. These experiences will appear to that future life as if they were memories of past lives, spiritual seeds waiting to be germinated upon their rediscovery. Once the monadic-soul has attained a high enough level of development, it will be able to trigger this kind of projection to reinforce key events in its future evolution.

Note 28. Even before this kind of capacity has fully developed, the dreaming-soul may still receive glimpses of the monadic-soul's own experiences that are occurring while the monadic-soul is in the process of peering into its life. For example, the reactions experienced by the monadic-soul while viewing events in the future life may appear to the dreaming-soul as if they were its own thoughts.

Note 29. Because the soul-spirit is the source of the awareness of dreaming-souls as well as that of the monadic-soul, some amount of the experiences of the visiting monadic-soul will always be transmitted to the experiences of these future, still dreaming, souls, creating a dynamic feedback loop that ripples wave-like throughout the Multi-Soul. The channel of awareness, when open, will be open in both directions, due to the power of spiritual entanglement.

Note 30. The innate receptivity of the monadic-soul to the experiences of dreaming-souls living in other parallel realms is the source of its ability to expand its experience and accelerate its development. But this same receptivity also makes it vulnerable to incursions by forces and energies from outside the evolutionary track in the Multi-Soul. It is important to the monadic-soul's development that it learns how to differentiate and discard those alien and potentially hostile experiences.

Note 31. This process of sequentially lived lives with its incumbent cycles of death and rebirth will continue until the fragmentation of the spirit is repaired. This will only occur when the monadic-soul is able to establish full, two-way communication with enough of its remaining future selves in the Multi-Soul to trigger a spiritual chain reaction, leading to a reunification event. At that point all of the fragmented souls will share complete consciousness with each other, becoming fully integrated into one unified monadic-soul, simultaneously alive with full awareness on multiple planes of being.

## Visions and the Etheric Body

The following notes on the nature of the etheric body and its connection to visions are the results of an extended period of energetic experiences that began approximately three months after I began to meditate, following a period during which I received several dozen of visions spanning multiple worlds. I experienced two distinct forms of energies, one a spiraling vertical energy traveling up and down a central channel and the other various kinds of rotating energies that flowed in smaller or larger circuits, some in front of the central channel and one on each side. In addition, one appeared at the top of the central channel, circulating halo-like above the head.

Of particular relevance to this section were six distinct vortexes of energy (chakras) that rotated at different levels perpendicular to the central channel in front of the torso in alternating clockwise (CW) and counter-clockwise (CCW) directions. When active, these served as gateways to outflows (CW) and inflows (CWW) of energies. From the Taoist point of view, outflowing CW energy represents active Yang energy, while inflowing CCW is receptive Yin energy.

Note 32. Within an incarnation, the monadic-soul is connected to its physical embodiment via the energetic channels and gateways of the etheric body. This etheric body is the medium through which experiences received from the physical world receive illumination and projection into consciousness. Because it is formed of soul stuff, it is also the medium through which transmissions pass between the monadic-soul and the other dreaming-souls alive in other realms.

Note 33. Communications between these other realms can take many forms, but only those vivid enough to form memories will be able to be recalled and later reviewed within waking consciousness. The strongest forms of other-life perception will occur as visions during meditation or in the form of special life-like kinds of dreams. On rare occasions these may also overlay experiences of the mundane waking world, the result of a superposition occurring between the mundane and spiritual world.

Note 34. There are multiple ways in which other lives can be experienced within a vision, ranging from simple witnessing as a disembodied observer all the way up to assuming the identity of the alternative self. In the latter case you would not only see through their eyes and think their thoughts, you would literally be them as long as the vision lasted. This same phenomenon will also occur in those dreams in which you were experiencing another lifetime.

Note 35. Because visions from other lifetimes are received through the mediation of the etheric body, an energetic component accompanies the visual and symbolic content experienced within consciousness. This energetic component is in fact the source of the experienced content, through its interaction with the etheric body and subsequent generation of mental images and memories.

Note 36. Just as the content of visionary experiences can lead to intellectual and emotional change, the energetic component of visions can also impact the functional elements of the etheric body, especially with respect to the channels and gateways governing their reception.

Note 37. Like water flowing downhill carves channels that guide its passage and sweeps away obstacles impeding its course, so too will streams of visions received from other worlds gradually widen the channels and gateways in the etheric body that provide access to them in the current incarnation.

Note 38. One of the most important correspondences between the nature of a vision's content and the components of the etheric body involves the notion of visionary world levels. In many different spiritual traditions, visions have been found to occur on one of three different world levels. This observation points to the existence of similar levels within the vertical channel running up the center of the etheric body.

Note 39. Multiple traditions have identified six energy gateways or nodes (sometimes called "chakras") occurring in the etheric body that correspond to the following locations on the front of the physical body: the forehead, the throat, the heart, the sternum, the navel, and the lower abdomen. These gateways emerge at a right angle from an energy channel running vertically along the spinal column of the body, which has two gateways at its end points, one at the crown of the head (the "Bai Hui" acupuncture point) and the other at the perineum or bottom-most point of the torso (the "Hui Yin" point).

Note 40. Each of the three visionary world levels, lower, surface (middle), and upper, are related to sequentially paired gateways, with each pair constituting a gateway hub:

| GATEWAY CORRESPONDENCES | | |
|---|---|---|
| WORLD LEVEL | GATEWAY HUB | LOCATION |
| Upper | Upper | Forehead |
| | | Throat |
| Surface (Middle) | Middle | Heart |
| | | Sternum |
| Lower | Lower | Navel |
| | | Lower Abdomen |

Note 41. The gateway hubs are paired because for optimal communication, one gateway would be outgoing and the other incoming, forming a circular flow of energy via its channels to the other world realms and back to the etheric body. In one channel the monadic-soul would send its awareness out to merge with the dreaming-soul on its world. In the other it would transmit the experiences it witnessed back to its etheric body.

Note 42. Since consciousness (or Yang) energy travels in an upward direction in the central core of the etheric body, smooth energy flow between worlds would occur when the lower gateway of each level's pair governed the outgoing (Yang energy) channel and the upper gateway the incoming (Yin energy) channel.

Note 43. When energies were perfectly balanced, the following relationships would occur:

| IDEAL ENERGY CONFIGURATIONS | | | |
|---|---|---|---|
| HUB | GATEWAY | ENERGY | DIRECTION |
| Upper World | Forehead | Yin | In |
| Upper World | Throat | Yang | Out |
| Surface (Middle) World | Heart | Yin | In |
| Surface (Middle) World | Sternum | Yang | Out |
| Lower World | Navel | Yin | In |
| Lower World | Lower Abdomen | Yang | Out |

Note 44. Because every vision embodies its own specific configuration of energy, each vision will have a different impact on the relative efficacy of the three gateway hubs and their connected channels. One type of vision may have no impact on any gateway or channel, while another may serve to further energize one or more gateways. Some may only contribute to a channel's throughput while others might boost throughput for both a channel and a gateway.

Note 45. For most individuals, the channels and gateways of the nodal hubs would remain in an occluded state, allowing only minimal levels of communication between worlds, probably occurring in deep dream states. Opening the gateways and keeping them open would require an influx and buildup of the right kind of energies. Similarly, the channels would need a more continuous flow of energies to keep them open and increase the amount of their throughput.

Note 46. The full process of hub activation will require repeated cycles of energetic stimulation from the experience of visions expressing the proper configurations of Yin and Yang energies. Once a full cycle of activation has occurred within a given incarnation, the monadic-soul will have established channels of connection between multiple other lives and realms, sharing a wide spectrum of experiences and consciousness with them.

Note 47. These open channels will enable the monadic-soul, when it moves into its next incarnation, to begin its life with not only a higher level of access to knowledge from the previous incarnation, but also a pre-established set of connections to the future lives contacted in this prior incarnation as well. As a result, this next life will embody a more highly evolved monadic-soul and a stronger sense of continuity between lifetimes.

Note 48. Fuller unification of the monadic-soul will require this process to be repeated many times over many lifetimes, until a sufficiently critical mass of interconnections among the universe of future incarnations has been accomplished to create a spiritual chain reaction that will rapidly spread throughout the Multi-Soul.

Note 49. The form of consciousness that would be displayed by a monadic-soul that has achieved full unification throughout the Multi-Soul is, of course, way beyond the ability of the limited non-illuminated mind to understand. Prior to illumination, it could not comprehend what it would be like to be fully awake and aware within multiple lifetimes simultaneously.

Note 50. While the existence of highly evolved souls outside the realm of normal human experience has been documented throughout history, even those individuals fell far short of the kind of extended, multi-life consciousness that would be possible for the fully illuminated soul envisioned here, one probably more godlike in its abilities than human.

# The I-Ching and the Spectral Soul

Like so many of my new beliefs, the impetus for discovering a correlation between the imagery of the ancient Chinese classic of divination, the I-Ching, and the implicit symbolism within the monadic-soul's experiences of the visionary realms, was contained within the visions themselves. The system that King Wen developed in the I-Ching to analyze the forces driving the processes of change between events can also be used to identify the energetic contribution of visions to the activation of the inter-life gateways.

## The I Ching

Note 51. The I-Ching, translated as "Book of Changes," is a highly symbolic work of divination. It is based on the analysis of the implications of a six-lined pictogram (a hexagram) to a particular situation facing an individual. The individual, having formulated a question about the future, derived the pictogram by following a set of ritualized procedures involving the repeated counting of sticks or coins.

Note 52. The I-Ching's analysis of the resulting pictogram, "gua" in Chinese, provided a judgment regarding the relative favorability of the situation facing the individual and recommendations concerning the best strategy for the individual to pursue in that situation. The situation was regarded as evolving over a series of six stages, with each line ("yao") of the hexagram associated with one of the stages.

## Yin and Yang

Note 53. The Chinese philosophy of Yin-Yang is at the root of the I-Ching. Yin and Yang represent forces in the natural world that appear to be polar opposites of each other. But, in fact, they are complementary forces that constitute a unified, evolving, and dynamic system. As one polarity went to the extreme, it would turn into its opposite. Neither force was ever entirely pure. Each always contained some amount of its opposite. These two forces are customarily known as the "T'ai Chi" (literally, "the great polarity") but are also referred to as "Liang Yi" ("the two forms").

Note 54. The traditional Chinese characters for Yin and Yang represent respectively the shady and the sunny sides of a hill. It is one and the same hill. Only the illumination has changed. The modern characters use the example of the illumination from the moon and the sun for these same concepts.

Note 55. The contrasting energies of Yin and Yang are associated with many different examples of polarities:

| YIN | YANG |
|---|---|
| 阴 | 阳 |
| Place of the Moon | Place of the Sun |
| 蔭 | 暘 |
| Shady Side of Hill | Sunny Side of Hill |
| ▬ ▬ | ▬▬▬ |
| Female | Male |
| Earth | Heaven |
| Soul | Spirit |
| Anima | Animus |
| Unconscious | Conscious |
| Hidden | Manifest |
| Night | Day |
| Dark | Light |
| Respond | Initiate |
| Yielding | Firm |
| Down | Up |
| Cold | Hot |
| Withdraw | Emerge |
| Inwards | Outwards |
| Counter-CW (CCW) | Clockwise (CW) |
| Left | Right |
| Weak | Strong |
| Negative (−) | Positive (+) |
| 2 (Even numbers) | 1 (Odd numbers) |

Note 56. From the concept of the two starting polarities Yin and Yang, an additional dimension can be added to symbolically represent the cyclic relationship that existed between them, i.e., as one polarity of energy matured, it would transform into its opposite. Doubling the number of solid or broken lines in the original formulation created 4 possible states, called the "Four Symbols" ("Si Xiang" in Chinese), which depicted this new dimension. The following diagram shows the process of its generation:

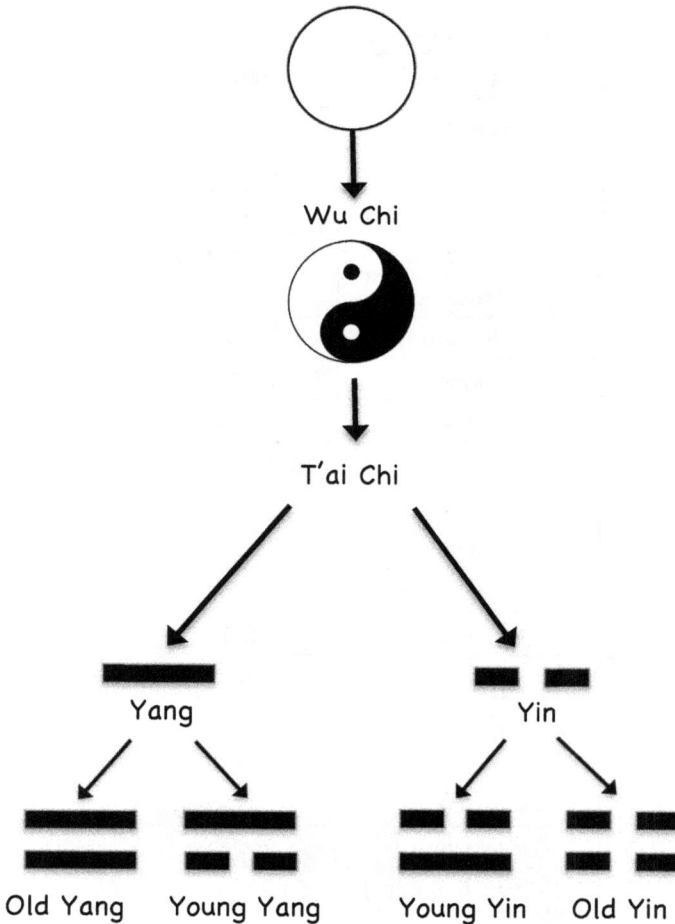

Wu Chi

T'ai Chi

Yang                                    Yin

Old Yang    Young Yang        Young Yin    Old Yin

Note 57. The more mature forms of the energies, Yin or Yang doubled, are labeled as "Old," indicating that they have reached their extreme and are already in the process of decline, ready to transform into their opposite. The younger versions, Young Yin and Yang, containing opposing forms of energy, are more balanced. The dynamic interaction of the two opposing forces creates a more powerful energy. Of the two, Young Yin is more potent, because a harmonic resonance is created by the interaction of the rising Yang with the falling Yin energies:

| Young Yang | Young Yin |
|---|---|

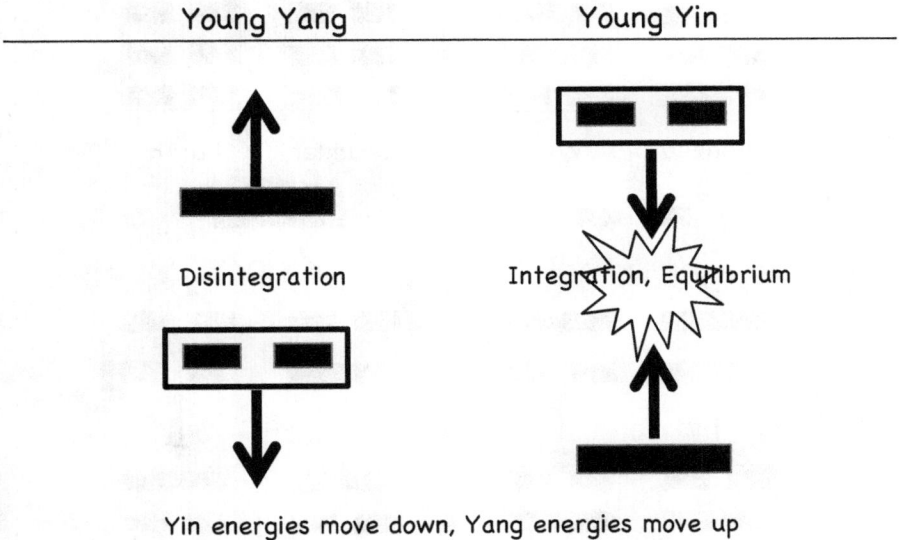

Disintegration                Integration, Equilibrium

Yin energies move down, Yang energies move up

## Trigrams and the Ba Gua

Note 58. The concept of Yin and Yang is further developed in the related concept of "Ba Gua" (literally, "eight symbols") that is used in Taoist philosophy to represent the fundamental, abstract principles of reality. These take the form of eight trigrams made of different stacked combinations of three solid or broken horizontal lines.

Note 59. This philosophy depicts the process of the emergence of the Ba Gua energies from the Si Xiang as follows:

# Generation of Trigrams

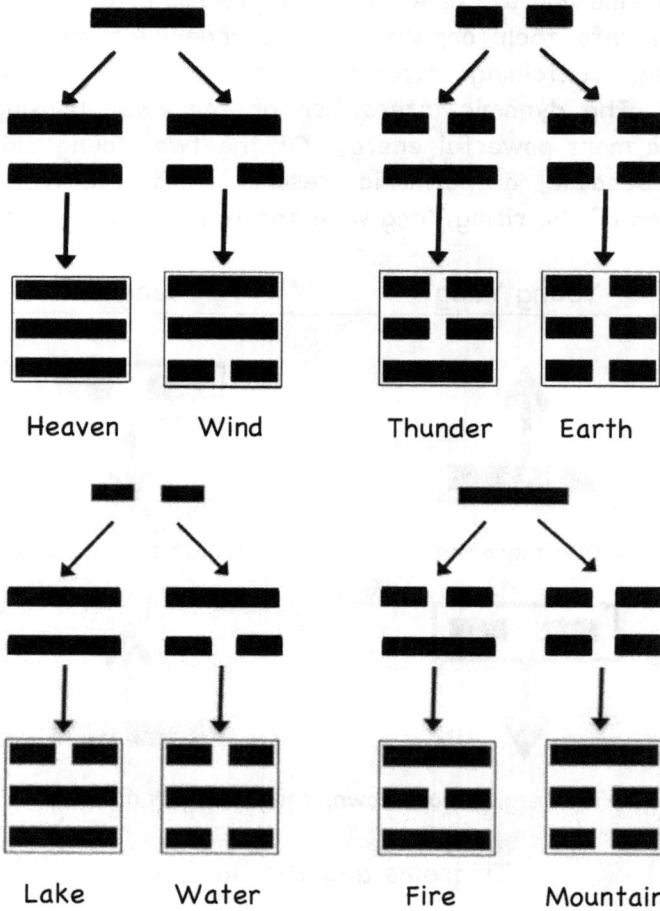

Heaven    Wind         Thunder    Earth

Lake    Water         Fire    Mountain

Note 60. The solid lines represent the Yang male principle, and the broken lines the female Yin principle. The different arrangements of these three lines can be used to signify distinct patterns of rising and falling energies as well as symbolic depictions of various natural phenomena for which they are named. The eight different forces are heaven, water, mountain, thunder, wind, fire, earth, and lake. These forces are also associated with an accompanying set of attributes, which will be described in greater detail in a subsequent section.

| NAME | SYMBOL | BINARY CODE | NUMBER (READ R TO L) |
|---|---|---|---|
| Heaven | | 111 | 7 |
| Water | | 010 | 2 |
| Mountain | | 100 | 4 |
| Thunder | | 001 | 1 |
| Wind | | 110 | 6 |
| Fire | | 101 | 5 |
| Earth | | 000 | 0 |
| Lake | | 011 | 3 |

Note 61. The mythological Chinese figure Fu Xi was reported to have invented this system of trigrams in the pre-historical epoch around 12,000 BC and created the first cyclic arrangement of them (the so-called Pre-Heaven arrangement) based on a pattern he saw on the back of a tortoise emerging from the Luo River.

Note 62. If the solid lines are viewed as 1 and the broken lines 0, Fu Xi can be seen as having inadvertently invented the binary number system. For example, the trigram named for mountain, which has a solid Yang line over two broken Yin lines, could be symbolized as the binary number (100), representing in binary code (reading from right to left) the decimal system number 4.

Note 63. These eight trigrams can be arranged in cyclical sequences of transformations. The two most well known arrangements represent in one case the configurations of energy prior to the creation of the universe and in the other the circulation of energies after the natural world and its "ten thousand things" were created.

Note 64. The Fu Xi sequence, the Pre-Heaven arrangement, shows a perfectly balanced and harmonious configuration of energies, with each trigram directly situated across from its opposite. Because of this balance, this configuration was completely static, existing before the beginning of time. Clockwise, from the top, the Pre-Heaven sequence goes as follows: heaven, wind, water, mountain, earth, thunder, fire, and lake. In these pairings each trigram's lines are the opposite of those in its mate.

Note 65. The other sequence is the Post-Heaven arrangement, which only came into existence once movement and time had begun. It depicts the dynamic ebb and flow of energy in the cycles of the natural world, such as the changes occurring during the four seasons of the year, the changing light of the sun in its passage from day to night, or the phases of the moon over a month. The focus of this arrangement was not the pairings of opposing trigrams, but the flow of energies throughout a cycle, as one configuration of energies transformed into the next due to the different interchanges of Yin and Yang energies. Clockwise, from the top, the Post-Heaven sequence goes as follows: fire, earth, lake, heaven, water, mountain, thunder, and wind.

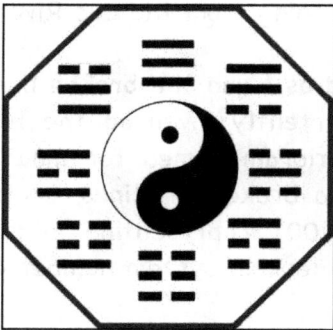

Pre-Heaven Arrangement          Post-Heaven Arrangement

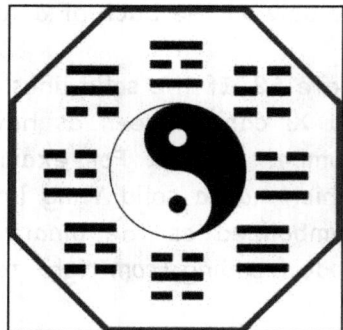

# The Hexagrams (Gua)

Note 66. The creation of the Post-Heaven arrangement was attributed to King Wen of the Zhou dynasty (around 1100 BC). In addition to this arrangement, King Wen was credited with having arranged all the eight trigrams in groupings of two each by stacking one upon the other, resulting in the creation of sixty-four different hexagrams ("gua" in Chinese), which he arranged in a distinctive ordering. Why he chose the over-all order he did still remains a mystery.

Note 67. Besides creating the ordering of these sixty-four hexagrams, King Wen gave them each a name that captured the essence of the situation they represented. He also included a short judgment about the nature of the decision that confronted people in that situation. This material forms the core of the King Wen I-Ching.

Note 68. Popular editions of the I-Ching supplement King Wen's work with other commentaries. The most common set, attributed to his son (the Duke of Zhou), provided a judgment for each line ("yao" in Chinese) of the hexagram, based on the assumption that every situation evolved over six stages.

Note 69. Rather than interpret the six lines of the hexagram as referring to the stages of an evolving situation, this work will take a different approach. The fact that I experienced six different energy gateways during meditation sessions suggested a different kind of meaning for the symbolism of the six lines of the I-Ching hexagram.

Note 70. But this was not the only connection between the I-Ching and my visions that I experienced. In particular, it took a particular vision to reinforce the possible relationship between the I-Ching hexagrams and visionary content, though I did not realize it at the time. This connection stemmed from a common procedure used to derive a hexagram. In the vision "The Spirit Dancers," one of my earliest, I saw mixed groups of men and women standing six across on a stair-like platform that was three rows deep.

Note 71. Probably the most common method for deriving an I-Ching hexagram uses three coins. In this method, which determines one line at a time, the coins would be tossed. The resulting combination of heads and tails would identify whether the line was solid or broken.

Note 72. For example, one approach equates three tails with an Old Yang line, three heads with an Old Yin line, two tails with a Young Yin line, and two heads with a Young Yang line. The "older" designation indicates that the energies are near the end of their cycles and about to revert to the opposite form. For example, Old Yang would revert to Young Yin. Similarly, when Young Yin matured, it would turn into Old Yin.

Note 73. It wasn't until much later that I realized the correspondence between that vision and the three-coin method. This connection became apparent when I realized that I could view the gender of each individual within the vision as corresponding to a coin toss. A man would equal a "tail" and a woman a "head" (or vice versa). By moving from right to left for each of the six positions and counting the relative numbers of men and women from the three rows, I could derive a hexagram based on the coin technique.

Note 74. Even though I did not realize it at the time, this early vision was giving me an important clue, symbolically presenting me with a specific hexagram hidden within its content. This association between the vision and the I-Ching hexagram pointed to the possibility of directly associating a particular I-Ching hexagram with each one of my visions.

Note 75. The fact that I experienced sixty-four distinct visions following the initiation period described in MST only served to strengthen the significance of this correlation. In particular, it pointed to the possibility that there was a one-to-one correspondence between my visions and the sixty-four hexagrams of the I-Ching. My visionary journey took me on a complete circuit through the I-Ching hexagrams, though one that unfolded in a different order than that found in King Wen's I-Ching.

Note 76. While there would be many different dimensions of energy contained within a vision, one of these dimensions would explicitly address the contribution of its Yin or Yang energy component to each of the six levels of gateways and their associated channels. The relative contribution of a given vision to these gateways would be the result of the different configurations of these Yin and Yang energies found within the vision.

Note 77. Adopting the formalism of the I-Ching, this work will utilize a pictogram composed of six layers to symbolically represent the energetic contribution of a specific vision to the nodal hubs. Each layer will contain either a Yang (+) or a Yin (-) energy component, using the solid and broken lines of the I-Ching hexagram. This will result in a total of sixty-four different energy configurations that a given vision could assume.

Note 78. Based upon the relative arrangement of the Yin and Yang energies within the six positions, each one of the sixty-four configurations will make a different degree of contribution to the activation of the hubs and their channels. To quantify this contribution, I have developed a procedure for calculating an Activation Power Score for each of the sixty-four configurations.

Note 79. The establishment of a correspondence between the attributes of a given vision and one of these sixty-four energetic configurations will define a measure for that vision's contribution to the activation of the components within the hub system. This will allow the monadic-soul's progress towards full hub activation to be tracked as the seeker experiences a sequence of visions.

## Hexagram Scoring Criteria

Using tools from the I-Ching and analytical techniques for hexagram exegesis developed over centuries by scholars from various philosophical traditions, this section describes a method for assigning a relative power score to each of the 64 different hexagrams. Much of this section is developed from Alfred Huang's excellent study on the symbolism of the I-Ching (Huang, 2000).

Note 80. Scholars of the I-Ching have identified several criteria for evaluating the placement and relationships of the Yin and Yang energies within the different lines of the hexagram. These aspects determine each line's contributions to the overall energy dynamics of the hexagram and to the components of the energetic etheric body the hexagram represents. Many of these criteria stem from the respective properties of the Yin and Yang qualities of energy.

Note 81. Correctness. Chinese numerology associates odd numbers with the Yang lines and even numbers with the Yin. Each of the six positions in the hexagram is assigned a number with the count starting from the bottom of the stack, so the lowest position would be 1 and the next 2, and so on. So because the 1st, 3rd and 5th positions are odd, conditions are most favorable when solid Yang lines occupy those positions. Similarly, broken Yin lines should be present in the 2nd, 4th and 6th positions for the best outcome.

Note 82. Centrality. Centrality is another important property, especially for a central Yang line, which is regarded as more powerful than Yin, even when in a central Yin position. The 2nd and 5th positions are key because each represents the center of its respective trigram. The concept of being centered is essential to the Chinese concept of harmony and balance, especially within the Confucian tradition.

Note 83. Correspondence. The relationships of the 1st and 4th, 2nd and 5th, and 3rd and 6th lines are also significant, since they represent the same position in the upper and lower trigrams. The existence of this kind of correspondence establishes a linkage between the internal and external conditions represented by the upper and lower trigrams. In these pairs, balance is again sought. In the ideal state, one correctly placed Yin line is paired with one correctly placed Yang line.

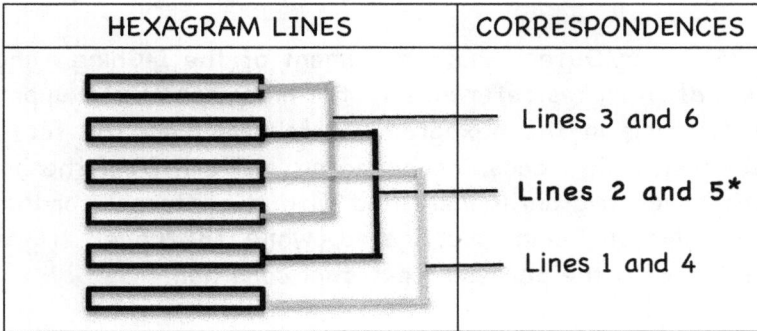

| HEXAGRAM LINES | CORRESPONDENCES |
|---|---|
| | Lines 3 and 6 |
| | Lines 2 and 5* |
| | Lines 1 and 4 |

\* The most important correspondence, since it
encompasses the central position of each trigram

Note 84. <u>Status</u>. Chinese philosophy also associated different levels of status with each of the positions in the hexagram, starting from the bottom up. The following chart shows these different status levels and their association with the Yin and Yang positions when they are in their correct places. Yang in the fifth position represents the strongest of all the lines, since it is associated with the role of the King.

| HEXAGRAM LINES | STAGE | ENERGY FLOW | CORRECTNESS | STATUS LEVELS |
|---|---|---|---|---|
| | 6 | | Yin | Sage |
| | 5* | | Yang* | King* |
| | 4 | ↑ | Yin | Minister |
| | 3 | | Yang | Lord |
| | 2 | | Yin | Official |
| | 1 | | Yang | Commoners |

\* The most significant line position

Note 85. <u>Carrying</u>. Because the presence of the 5<sup>th</sup> solid Yang line in a hexagram is so powerful, given that it is both centrally located and occupies the highest position of status, it is better for the neighboring 4<sup>th</sup> line to yield to the superior status of the 5<sup>th</sup>. The pairing of a Yin 4<sup>th</sup> line next to a Yang 5<sup>th</sup> line is accordingly viewed as a stabilizing factor for the hexagram.

Note 86. <u>Inner/Outer</u>. Another element of the I-Ching's analysis of a situation makes reference to the meanings of the upper and lower trigrams in the hexagram. It follows from the fact that Chinese philosophy reads the hexagram pattern from the bottom up. The lower trigram is identified with the internal condition of the phenomenon being investigated, while the upper trigram is associated with the perceived external condition.

Note 87. <u>Coherence</u>. Part of the overall evaluation of the hexagram therefore depends on the extent to which the external condition displayed by the outer trigram coherently expresses the hidden internal energies present in the lower trigram. From the standpoint of visionary analysis, the lower trigram represents the hidden forces of the unconscious (the inner spirit) and the upper trigram the manner in which these forces are manifested within the conscious experience of the vision (the external persona).

Note 88. <u>Transformation</u>. While the principles King Wen used to determine his macro-level ordering of the 64 hexagrams remain a mystery, at the micro-level his rule for the transformation between paired hexagrams is well known. Assuming a chapter number is assigned to each hexagram in the ordered sequence, the transition from an odd numbered hexagram to an even numbered one is always well defined. With the exception of a special type of hexagram, every even numbered hexagram is the result of applying an inversion transformation to the previous odd numbered one.

Note 89. <u>Inverted or Flipped Gua</u>. If you imagine a horizontal axis of rotation between the 3$^{rd}$ and 4$^{th}$ lines of the hexagram, an inversion transformation is the result of rotating the hexagram 180 degrees around this axis (i.e., turning it upside down). The complete set of transformations between lines would be as follows: 6 -> 1, 5 -> 2, 4 -> 3, 1 -> 6, 2 -> 5, and 3 -> 4. Note that in each case an odd numbered line would become an even numbered line and vice versa.

Note 90. <u>Symmetric Gua</u>. Eight special types of hexagrams exist that remain invariant under the inversion transformation. Because their upper and lower trigrams are reflected mirror images of each other, turning their hexagram upside down will produce no change. These eight hexagrams are perfectly symmetrical and balanced, representing a distinct type of equilibrium. For these kinds of hexagrams, the inner and outer trigrams would remain the same when inverted.

Note 91. <u>Reversed or Opposite Gua</u>. For this special class of symmetrical hexagrams, King Wen used a different kind of transformation to move from the odd to the even numbered hexagram. This was a reversal transformation, in which each line would be reversed to become the opposite in polarity, with a Yang line becoming a Yin one and a Yin line becoming a Yang one. This kind of transformation could be understood as resulting from a rotation through a mirrored dimension around the vertical axis.

Note 92. <u>Mutual Gua</u>. Besides the inversion and reversal transformation, there is another type that has been widely discussed in the I-Ching literature. This is the transformation that is used to derive a new hexagram from the central four places of the starting hexagram, usually called the "mutual gua" but also called by others the "nuclear gua" or the "middle gua." To create the new hexagram, lines 2, 3 & 4 are used to form a new lower trigram and lines 3, 4 & 5 to form the new upper trigram. According to its proponents, this new mutual hexagram will contain the inner meaning of the original hexagram because of its center-based derivation.

Note 93. <u>Inner Root Gua</u>. While the concept of the mutual gua is interesting, I believe there is another type of transformation that better captures the inner essence of a particular hexagram, which I call the "root" transformation. This type of transformation is based on the principle of mutuality, an expression of the co-mingled nature of Yin and Yang energies, as shown, for example, in the famous T'ai Chi diagram:

Note 94. For this transformation the hexagram is decomposed into its inner Yang and inner Yin trigram components by extracting the two sets of hexagram lines that are inherently Yang or inherently Yin in nature according to the correctness criteria. The inner Yang trigram, which would become the new lower trigram, would be composed of the odd numbered lines 1, 3 & 5. Similarly, the inner Yin trigram, the new upper one, would contain lines 2, 4, & 6. The two root trigrams exist in a co-mingled form within the original hexagram, a manifestation of one of the most basic properties of the Yin-Yang relationship.

Note 95. <u>Root Cycles</u>. Another important property of Yin and Yang that is seen in the T'ai Chi diagram is the manner in which the two energies dynamically cycle between each other. Examples of cycles are also found in the concept of the inner root gua. Unlike the mutual gua, the inner root gua will form cycles that will always return back to the starting hexagram.

Note 96. No matter from which hexagram you start, if you compute successive root gua's, you will eventually return to the starting hexagram. There are 24 different cycles that can be found, 8 of which are identities, 4 cycles that take 2 steps, and 12 cycles that take 4 steps before returning to the original hexagram. (See Appendixes H and I)

# Transformations on Hexagrams (Gua)

## Rotated around horizontal central axis

Inverse
(Flipped)
Gua

#3                                #4

## Yin and Yang are reversed on vertical axis

Opposite
(Reversed)
Gua

#3                                #50

## Lines 2,3,4 become new bottom, 3,4,5 new top

Mutual
(Center)
Gua

#3                                #23

## Lines 1,3,5 become new bottom, 2,4,6 new top

Inner
Root
Gua

#3                                #36

Note 97. Several examples in which two of these transformations are combined can be seen in the Post-Heaven trigram sequence:

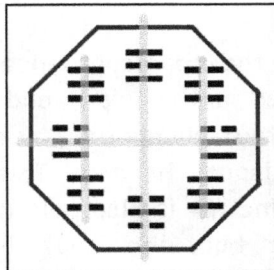

The three vertical lines and the horizontal line added to this diagram depict combined inversion and reversal transformations.

## The Hub Activation Process

Using these criteria for evaluating the equilibrium and energy qualities of the different hexagrams, higher order criteria for assessing the relative contributions of different hexagrams to the activation of the hub gateways and channels for inter-life communication can be developed.

Note 98. Within the six layers of the hexagram, the bottom two will correspond to the lower gateway hub, the center two the middle gateway hub, and the top two the upper gateway hub. Depending on the configuration of the Yin and Yang energies represented by the hexagram, each of these hubs will receive different amounts of activation energy.

Note 99. A necessary condition for a gateway hub to be regarded as potentially able to receive experiences from other lives is that the line representing its upper input channel in the hexagram be in the receptive Yin mode. Accordingly, for the lower hub, line #2 must be Yin, for the middle hub, line #4, and for the upper hub, line #6.

Note 100. Similarly, for experiences to be available for receipt by the input channels, the consciousness of the monadic-soul must be able to reach out to these other lives via the lower output channels. That would require that the line representing the lower input channel for a hub in the hexagram must be in the active Yang mode. For the lower hub, line #1 must be Yang, for the middle hub, line #3, and for the upper hub, line #5.

Note 101. Because of the correspondence that exists between similarly positioned lines in the upper and lower trigrams, there exists an additional output channel that can be paired with each of the odd numbered input channels. This means that, for the middle hub, the input line #4 is also paired with the Yang output line #1, for the upper hub, the input line #6 with the Yang output line #3, and for purposes of completeness, the input line #2 with the Yang output line #5.

Note 102. As a result, for each one of the three hub input channels, there are two output channels available for its activation. One active output channel will be sufficient for establishing some degree of consciousness of the experience of another life, but two will be required to both establish the linkage and provide sufficient bandwidth for returning elements of that experience back to the input channel.

Note 103. If only one output channel is active, that will be termed a "channel activation event." If two are active, that will be a "gateway activation event." A gateway activation event is equivalent to two channel activation events occurring within the same hexagram.

Note 104. An analysis of the levels of hub activation provided by the configurations of the sixty-four different hexagrams reveals that hub activation is a process occurring over multiple stages. This is due to the need for continuing energy flow to not only fully open channels and their associated gateways, but also to keep them open. For each hub to be fully activated, 16 channel activation events and 8 gateway activation events will be required.

Note 105. Activation Power Score. A hexagram Activation Power Score will represent the level of contribution made by each hexagram towards hub activation. This Activation Score, which will count the number of activation events associated with a given hexagram, will range between 0 and 6.

Note 106. Hub Activation Level. At each point in the cycle, a Hub Activation Level, which tabulates the number of channel and gateway activation events that have occurred for each hub, will represent the current level of hub activation.

Note 107. Hexagram Power Score. By combining the Activation Power Score with the hexagram scoring criteria, an aggregate Hexagram Power Score for each hexagram will be obtained. The score is calculated by using the following Power Scoring Matrix and will range in practice between 1 and 15. For comparison purposes, a quartile Power Score will also be reported for each hexagram, with the first quartile being the highest score.

| CORRECTNESS | 1 point per match, max 6 |
|---|---|
| Yang+ for Lines 1, 3, 5 | |
| Yin- for Lines 2, 4, 6 | |
| | |
| ACTIVATION PAIRS | 1 point per match, max 6 |
| Lower: (1+, 2-), (5+, 2-) | |
| Middle: (3+, 4-), (1+, 4-) | |
| Upper: (5+, 6-), (3+. 6-) | |
| | |
| CARRYING | 1 point for match |
| Yin- Line 4, Yang+ Line 5 | |
| | |
| CENTRALITY | 1 point for match, max 2 |
| Yang+ Line 2 | |
| Yang+ Line 5 | |
| Yin- Line 2 if Yang+ Line 5 | |
| | |
| REFLECTIVE SYMMETRY | 1 point for match |
| If top gua mirrors bottom | |
| | |

Note 108. <u>Hexagram Total Dual Score</u>. Because of the significance of the inner root gua hidden within each hexagram, a combined score, the Total Dual Score, along with an associated quartile score, will also be calculated for each hexagram, by adding the Inner Root Gua's Power Score to the hexagram's own Power Score. In practice, Total Dual Scores will range from a low of 3 to a high of 24. This score will represent the total amount of energy available for hub activation associated with a given hexagram.

Note 109. The project of matching each one of sixty-four visions in their narrative order with a unique hexagram will define a complete cycle of hub activation. Any specific sequence for moving through the sixty-four hexagrams is a unique map of the stages by which the series of three gateway hubs can be activated.

Note 110. While King Wen in the I-Ching presented an arrangement of the sixty-four different hexagrams based on his observations of the patterns and cyclic movements of natural phenomenon, the sequence of sixty-four visions will result in the creation of a distinctive ordering of the energetic route traveled by the monadic-soul in the process of actualizing the full capacities of its etheric body. Because full hub gateway activation is a key step in the awakening and ultimate liberation of the monadic-soul, it is also a description of the soul's transformative journey of liberation in this lifetime.

Note 111. In the same way that each person is the embodiment of a distinctive DNA sequence, with no two people having the same sequence (unless, of course, they are identical twins), so too will the resulting hexagram sequence be a unique signature defining the characteristics of a person's distinct psychic life. This sequence describes the cycle of the soul's transformations and, for all individuals, is a description of their gDNA sequence, or "gateway Dynamic Node Activation sequence."

Note 112. This gDNA sequence defines the alchemical process of transformation that occurs in the process of the etheric body's development, just as DNA encodes the blueprints for the physical body's development. The gDNA encodes all the potential responses and drives and reactions of the etheric body to the spectrum of events and experiences that will occur during its lifetime.

Note 113. If the gDNA sequence for a particular incarnation defines the spiritual genome of the monadic-soul at a particular stage in its evolution, then the evolution of the monadic-soul and its drive for liberation can be seen as the transformation of its underlying gDNA sequence, as changes to it, representative of spiritual growth, slowly accumulate over the course of a multitude of lifetimes.

Note 114. Just as structured segments of genes in DNA encode for proteins, which are the body's functional components, the narratives than can be identified within sequences of visions define discrete groupings of gDNA sequences. These groupings, which I call "narrative genes" or "nGenes," have both a spiritual component, directed at completing specific stages of spiritual growth, as well as an energetic functional component, which accumulates sufficient energy to fuel transformative change by removing blockages in the flow of energy in the etheric body.

Note 115. In most cases a narrative's content occurs within the domain of a particular world realm. It is usually experienced either from the point of view of the subject living in that world or shown to the seeker sitting in meditation through the auspices of a spiritual teacher or mentor present in that realm.

Note 116. This means that the sequence of energy configurations defining a particular nGene are active both in the current incarnation's etheric body as well as in that of the future incarnation where these defining visions are being experienced. The fact that the same sequence occurs in two different lifetimes indicates the nGene has been conserved in the course of the gDNA's process of evolution through these multiple lifetimes.

Note 117. The underlying process of gDNA evolution driving the monadic-soul's journey of liberation determines which lifetimes will be visited and which vision's experienced within a particular incarnation. Only those lifetimes can be witnessed which contain nGene sequences sufficiently similar to ones existing in the current incarnation.

Note 118. The gDNA sequences of the future lives must contain nGene components that will be conserved in the course of development from the present life to the future one. And more importantly, whatever elements of their gDNA genome are different from the current one must represent changes that will move the gDNA closer to a state supportive of future spiritual liberation.

Note 119. The mathematically inclined reader will note that there are a total of 64 factorial (64!) ways of sequencing the 64 different hexagrams or 1.26886932 X 10 to the 89th power, which is reported to be far more than the number of atoms in the entire known Universe.

Note 120. While the likelihood of any two people coming up with identical gDNA configurations would be nil, even between incarnations of the same monadic-soul, the more interesting question would be the extent to which people would share nGene segments with matching sequences, much as humans do in the case of DNA.

Note 121. The ability of the monadic-soul in a given lifetime to witness specific kinds of experiences from other lifetimes indicates that nGene sequences have been conserved between these two lifetimes. The fact that certain kinds of visionary experiences have appeared throughout history across many different spiritual traditions suggests that matching nGene sequences might be representative of a more general principle. In particular, it suggests a basis for the type of archetypal complexes postulated by Jung as having evolved in our collective unconscious.

# I Ching Trigram Interpretation

While the I-Ching and its collection of hexagrams are traditionally viewed as a manual for divination, I will be using it as a tool to help identify hidden patterns of meaning in each vision and to identify the energetic transformations underway in the etheric body. For each vision I will identify a unique hexagram that I believe best expresses the underlying meaning of the vision.

## The Soul's Transformative Journey

In this section I will go into much greater detail on the different levels of meaning contained within each trigram and on the ways in which their combination will result in a hexagram definitive of a distinctive type of life experience. The process of identifying which hexagram should be associated with each vision will need to take into account all these different interpretative layers in order to find the best match.

It is my hope that over time the reader will come to see the reasons behind my choices as well as gain some fluency in recognizing the different trigram patterns and their associations, though, of course, as this occurs, they may (and probably should) begin to entertain their own alternative associations and interpretations as well.

Note 122. On one level, these hexagrams will act as signposts for a meditative practice and annotate the state of its progress through the labyrinth of the monadic-soul's other worlds and lifetimes. The resulting new sequence of hexagrams that emerge from this analysis will serve as a unique map of the monadic-soul's own distinct journey through the hidden regions of the Multi-Soul.

Note 123. On a deeper level, the sequence of these hexagrams will represent the on-going process of energetic transformation and gateway activation underway in the etheric body as the monadic-soul samples the experiences of a selection of future lifetimes with the goal of triggering alchemical transformations in its current incarnation.

Note 124. Sometimes, based on the symbolic imagery present within the vision, an immediate association with two trigrams will naturally occur, leading to the particular hexagram that results from their juxtaposition. For example, the imagery in a vision of light burrowing deep into the ground will represent the symbolism of earth over fire, leading directly to the I-Ching hexagram #36, Brilliance Concealed.

Note 125. Other times the association of a particular hexagram with a vision will be based on the fit between the interpretation of the vision and that of the hexagram, as expressed by the figurative name given it in the I-Ching and the attributes and qualities that can be associated with its trigrams. For example, a vision showing a mass of people running from a perceived danger is a literal expression of the name for hexagram #33, Retreat.

## The Five Phases (Elements)

Note 126. One of the qualities associated both with trigrams and hexagrams involves the Chinese belief that there exist five fundamental forces or kinds of elemental phase transitions that drive the cycles and transformations of a wide array of natural phenomenon. The type of force associated with the hexagram will be derived from the one associated with its upper trigram.

Note 127. The Chinese philosophy of forces is found in the so-called Five Element theory ("Wu Xing"), where wood, metal, water, earth, and fire, are the fundamental forces. The customary translation of "Five Elements" isn't strictly correct, since "xing" should be translated as "phases," resulting in the translation "Five Phases."

| THE 五 FIVE 行 PHASES | | | | |
|---|---|---|---|---|
| WOOD | FIRE | EARTH | METAL | WATER |
| Mu | Huo | Tu | Jin | Shui |
| 木 | 火 | 土 | 金 | 水 |
| Tree, Wood | Fire, Urgent, Heat | Earth, Dust, Clay | Gold, Lustrous Metals | Water, River, Liquid |

Note 128. In Chinese martial arts we regard these five elemental transitions as different configurations and vectors of energy discharge, where wood is horizontally penetrating like an arrow, metal is vertically chopping down like an ax, fire is exploding upwards like a cannon, earth is horizontally winding like a river bed, and water is vertically falling and rising in circular patterns like a wave.

Note 129. The *Yellow Emperor's Classic of Internal Medicine* describes these energies as follows: "Wood refers to expansion and harmony, fire refers to rising and illumination, earth refers to completeness and transformation, metal refers to alignment and leveling, water refers to quiet and obedience."

Note 130. Other schools of Chinese philosophy describe a relationship between the concepts of Si Xiang, the Four Symbols, as they are expressed within the trigrams, and the Five Phases. Multiple dimensions of correlation are established, including those between the four cardinal directions of the compass (and a central point), the four seasons, and a set of mythical Beings.

| PHASE | GUA | SYMBOL | SEASON | DIRECTION | BEING |
|-------|-----|--------|--------|-----------|-------|
| Wood | ☳ | Young Yin | Spring | East | Azure Dragon |
| Fire | ☲ | Young Yin | Summer | South | Vermillion Bird |
| Metal | ☱ | Old Yang | Fall | West | White Tiger |
| Water | ☵ | Young Yang | Winter | North | Black Warrior |
| Earth | ☷ | Old Yin | N/A | Center | Yellow Dragon |

Note 131. These four cardinal directions correspond to the compass locations on King Wen's Post-Heaven arrangement of the trigrams, when you understand that the Chinese compass was one that had been rotated 180 degrees from ours.

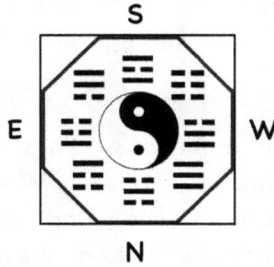

Note 132. While this set of Beings is traditionally referred to as mythological, I can testify that I experienced each one of them in the course of my visions, leading to me to believe that Chinese mystics had seen them as well and that these images were visionary archetypes of primordial forms of energy configurations.

## Associations with Trigram Levels

Note 133. The concept of the triad or trichotomy that is embodied in the Chinese trigram symbol has had many different expressions throughout the history of philosophy and religion. For traditional I-Ching interpretation, the three levels represented heaven and earth above and below, with humankind in the middle. The following table shows a sampling of some of the more prominent examples.

| SOURCE | TOP | MIDDLE | BOTTOM |
|---|---|---|---|
| I-Ching Trigram Line Levels | Heaven | Human | Earth |
| Taoist Inner Alchemy | Spirit (Shen) | Energy (Ch'i or Qi) | Essence (Jing) |
| Dan T'ian Fields | Upper | Middle | Lower |
| Plato | Rational | Libidinous | Spirited |
| Plotinus | The One | The Intellect | The Soul |
| St. Augustine | Intellect | Will | Memory |
| St. Paul | Spirit | Soul | Body |
| Kant | Knowledge | Pleasure | Desire |
| Freud | Superego | Ego | Id |
| Merleau-Ponty | Human | Vital | Physical |
| Gurdjieff | Intellectual | Emotional | Moving |
| Christianity | Father | Son | Holy Ghost |
| Hinduism | Brahma | Vishnu | Shiva |
| Aurobindo | Mental | Vital | Physical |
| Aurobindo | Psychic Being | Inner Being | Outer Being |
| The Brain | Neocortex | Limbic | Reptilian |

See "Trichotomy (Philosophy)" in *Wikipedia* for a more complete listing

Note 134. The trichotomy of the three-leveled psyche, as represented by the following diagram, is of particular relevance to trigram interpretation.

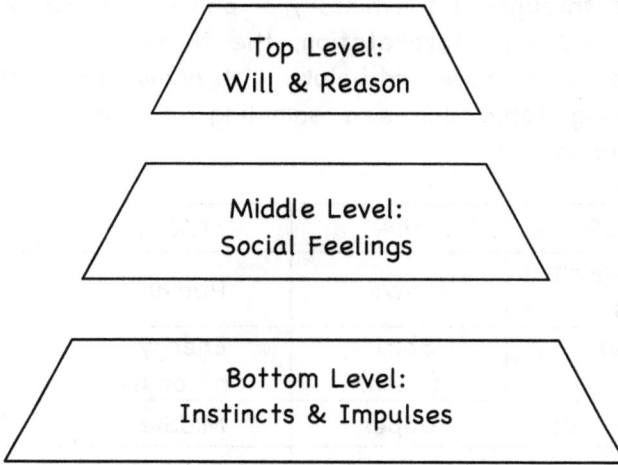

Top Level:
Will & Reason

Middle Level:
Social Feelings

Bottom Level:
Instincts & Impulses

Note 135. Using this model, the key psychological qualities that are associated with each of the eight trigrams can be derived:

| GUA | STATE | GUA | STATE |
|---|---|---|---|
| ☳ | Thunder<br>Pure Impulse =<br>Aroused | ☱ | Lake<br>Impulse + Feeling =<br>Passionate |
| ☵ | Water<br>Pure Feeling =<br>Immersed | ☴ | Wind<br>Feeling + Will =<br>Focused |
| ☶ | Mountain<br>Pure Will =<br>Stubborn | ☲ | Fire<br>Impulse + Will =<br>Excited |
| ☷ | Earth<br>Pure Passivity<br>= Yielding | ☰ | Heaven<br>Pure Engagement =<br>Engaged |

Note 136. The individual trigrams will have different power scores associated with them depending upon whether they are in the upper or lower positions in the hexagram. For the purpose of scoring the trigrams in the two positions, I will employ a truncated version of the Power Scoring Matrix. In particular, the middle activation node and correspondence based activation associations are disregarded, along with the symmetry reflection attribute.)

### Trigram Power Scoring Matrix

| **CORRECTNESS** | 1 point per match, max 3 per trigram |
|---|---|
| Yang+ for Lines 1, 3, 5 | |
| Yin- for Lines 2, 4, 6 | |
| | |
| **ACTIVATION PAIRS** | 1 point per match, max 1 per trigram |
| Lower:   (1+, 2) | |
| Upper:   (5+, 6-) | |
| | |
| **CARRYING** | 1 point for match, upper trigram only |
| Yin- Line 4, Yang+ Line 5 | |
| | |
| **CENTRALITY** | 1 point for match, max 1 per trigram |
| Yang+ Line 2 | |
| Yang+ Line 5 | |
| | |

Maximum score = 6 for upper trigram, 4 for lower

# The Eight Trigrams

The following section will present for each trigram its set of associated attributes, scoring matrices, and list of qualities that will be used in subsequent hexagram analysis.

# HEAVEN (INITIATING) TRIGRAM

☰

## QIAN 乾

| ATTRIBUTE | VALUE |
|---|---|
| Yin/Yang | Yang |
| Si Xiang | Old Yang |
| Family Member | Father |
| Correlates | Sky, Laws of Heaven |
| Element | Metal (Gold) |
| Density | Low |
| Temperature Change | Raise |
| Rate of Effect | Fast |
| Impact | Strong |
| Direction | Up |
| Illumination Impact | Increase |
| Psyche | Engaged |

## SCORING MATRIX

| Gua Diagram | Line | Correct | Active | Central | Carry |
|---|---|---|---|---|---|
| | 6 | 0 | 0 | | |
| | 5 | 1 | | 1 | 0 |
| | 4 | 0 | | | |
| | 3 | 1 | | | |
| | 2 | 0 | 0 | 1 | |
| | 1 | 1 | | | |

TOP POSITION SCORE: 2
BOTTOM POSITION SCORE: 3
TOP + BOTTOM SCORE: 5

## QUALITIES

Initiating, Powerful, Creative, Strong, Forceful, Advancing

# EARTH (RESPONDING) TRIGRAM

## KUN 坤

| ATTRIBUTE | VALUE |
|---|---|
| Yin/Yang | Yin |
| Si Xiang | Old Yin |
| Family Member | Mother |
| Correlates | Land, Field, Soil |
| Element | Earth |
| Density | High |
| Temperature Change | Lower |
| Rate of Effect | Slow |
| Impact | Weak |
| Direction | Down |
| Illumination Impact | Decrease |
| Psyche | Yielding |

### SCORING MATRIX

| Gua Diagram | Line | Correct | Active | Central | Carry |
|---|---|---|---|---|---|
| | 6 | 1 | 0 | | |
| | 5 | 0 | | 0 | 0 |
| | 4 | 1 | | | |
| | 3 | 0 | | | |
| | 2 | 1 | 0 | 0 | |
| | 1 | 0 | | | |

TOP POSITION SCORE: 2
BOTTOM POSITION SCORE: 1
TOP + BOTTOM SCORE: 3

## QUALITIES

Receptive, Responsive, Dormant, Nurturing, Compliant, Peaceful, Yielding, Buried

# WATER (DARKNESS) TRIGRAM

KAN 坎

| ATTRIBUTE | VALUE |
|---|---|
| Yin/Yang | Ying |
| Si Xiang | Young Yang |
| Family Member | Middle Son |
| Correlates | River, Rain, Clouds |
| Element | Water |
| Density | Moderate |
| Temperature Change | Lower |
| Rate of Effect | Slow |
| Impact | Strong |
| Direction | Down (Wavelike) |
| Illumination Impact | Decrease |
| Psyche | Immersed |

## SCORING MATRIX

| Gua Diagram | Line | Correct | Active | Central | Carry |
|---|---|---|---|---|---|
| | 6 | 1 | 1 | | |
| | 5 | 1 | | 1 | 1 |
| | 4 | 1 | | | |
| | 3 | 0 | | | |
| | 2 | 0 | 0 | 1 | |
| | 1 | 0 | | | |

TOP POSITION SCORE: 6 (HIGHEST)
BOTTOM POSITION SCORE: 1
TOP + BOTTOM SCORE: 7 (HIGHEST)

## QUALITIES

Dark, Flowing, Unstable, Engaged, Swimming, Immersed, Motion, Streaming, Flowing, Dangerous

# FIRE (BRIGHTNESS) TRIGRAM

## LI 離

| ATTRIBUTE | VALUE |
|---|---|
| Yin/Yang | Yang |
| Si Xiang | Young Yin |
| Family Member | Middle Daughter |
| Correlates | Fire, Lightning, Sun |
| Element | Fire |
| Density | Low |
| Temperature Change | Raise |
| Rate of Effect | Fast |
| Impact | Strong |
| Direction | Up |
| Illumination Impact | Increase |
| Psyche | Excited |

## SCORING MATRIX

| Gua Diagram | Line | Correct | Active | Central | Carry |
|---|---|---|---|---|---|
| | 6 | 0 | 0 | | |
| | 5 | 0 | | 0 | 0 |
| | 4 | 0 | | | |
| | 3 | 1 | | | |
| | 2 | 1 | 1 | 0 | |
| | 1 | 1 | | | |

TOP POSITION SCORE: 0
BOTTOM POSITION SCORE: 4 (HIGHEST)
TOP + BOTTOM SCORE: 4

## QUALITIES

Illuminated, Clinging, Consuming, Flaming, Enlightened, Climbing,
Excited, Inflamed, Brightness

# THUNDER (TAKING ACTION) TRIGRAM

## ZHEN 震

| ATTRIBUTE | VALUE |
|---|---|
| Yin/Yang | Yang |
| Si Xiang | Young Yin |
| Family Member | Eldest Son |
| Correlates | Explosion, Growth |
| Element | Wood |
| Density | Low |
| Temperature Change | Raise |
| Rate of Effect | Fast |
| Impact | Strong |
| Direction | Up / Sideways |
| Illumination Impact | Increase |
| Psyche | Aroused |

## SCORING MATRIX

| Gua Diagram | Line | Correct | Active | Central | Carry |
|---|---|---|---|---|---|
| | 6 | 1 | 0 | | |
| | 5 | 0 | | 0 | 0 |
| | 4 | 0 | | | |
| | 3 | 0 | | | |
| | 2 | 1 | 1 | 0 | |
| | 1 | 1 | | | |

TOP POSITION SCORE: 1
BOTTOM POSITION SCORE: 3
TOP + BOTTOM SCORE: 4

## QUALITIES

Rising, Aroused, Driven, Explosive, Action, Movement

# MOUNTAIN (KEEPING STILL) TRIGRAM

## GEN 艮

| ATTRIBUTE | VALUE |
|---|---|
| Yin/Yang | Yang |
| Si Xiang | Old Yin |
| Family Member | Youngest Son |
| Correlates | Mountain, Plateau |
| Element | Earth |
| Density | High |
| Temperature Change | Lower |
| Rate of Effect | Slow |
| Impact | Strong |
| Direction | Up |
| Illumination Impact | Decrease |
| Psyche | Stubborn |

## SCORING MATRIX

| Gua Diagram | Line | Correct | Active | Central | Carry |
|---|---|---|---|---|---|
| | 6 | 0 | 0 | | |
| | 5 | 0 | | 0 | 0 |
| | 4 | 1 | | | |
| | 3 | 1 | | | |
| | 2 | 1 | 0 | 0 | |
| | 1 | 0 | | | |

TOP POSITION SCORE: 1
BOTTOM POSITION SCORE: 2
TOP + BOTTOM SCORE: 3

## QUALITIES

Still, Bound, Tranquil, Stubborn, Obstructing, Stopped, Resistant, Aggregating, Blocked

# WIND (PROCEEDING HUMBLY) TRIGRAM

## XUN 巽

| ATTRIBUTE | VALUE |
|---|---|
| Yin/Yang | Yin |
| Si Xiang | Young Yang |
| Family Member | Eldest Daughter |
| Correlates | Wind, Trees, The Winged |
| Element | Wood |
| Density | Low |
| Temperature Change | Lower |
| Rate of Effect | Slow |
| Impact | Weak |
| Direction | Sideways / Down |
| Illumination Impact | Increase |
| Psyche | Focused |

## SCORING MATRIX

| Gua Diagram | Line | Correct | Active | Central | Carry |
|---|---|---|---|---|---|
| | 6 | 0 | 0 | | |
| | 5 | 1 | | 1 | 1 |
| | 4 | 1 | | | |
| | 3 | 1 | | | |
| | 2 | 0 | 0 | 1 | |
| | 1 | 0 | | | |

TOP POSITION SCORE: 4
BOTTOM POSITION SCORE: 2
TOP + BOTTOM SCORE: 6

## QUALITIES

Dispersed, Spreading, Scattered, Dissolution, Penetrating, Focused, Entering

# LAKE (JOYFUL) TRIGRAM

☱

## DUI 兌

| ATTRIBUTE | VALUE |
|---|---|
| Yin/Yang | Yin |
| Si Xiang | Old Yang |
| Family Member | Youngest Daughter |
| Correlates | Lake, Marsh, Ocean |
| Element | Metal (Silver) |
| Density | Moderate |
| Temperature Change | Lower |
| Rate of Effect | Slow |
| Impact | Weak |
| Direction | Down |
| Illumination Impact | Decrease |
| Psyche | Passionate |

## SCORING MATRIX

| Gua Diagram | Line | Correct | Active | Central | Carry |
|---|---|---|---|---|---|
| | 6 | 1 | 1 | | |
| | 5 | 1 | | 1 | 0 |
| | 4 | 0 | | | |
| | 3 | 0 | | | |
| | 2 | 0 | 0 | 1 | |
| | 1 | 1 | | | |

TOP POSITION SCORE: 4
BOTTOM POSITION SCORE: 2
TOP + BOTTOM SCORE: 6

## QUALITIES

Joyful, Deep, Passionate, Open, Emotional, Sinking

# A New Approach to the I-Ching

## The Traditional I-Ching

Most editions of the I-Ching that are currently available are variations on a theme. They all include the same collection of materials, usually supplemented with some additional discussion by the edition's author and translator. The translations of the Chinese content that is included will typically vary, depending on the philosophical outlook of the translator. In particular, the names given each hexagram are often quite different, and the names offered for certain hexagrams often contradict each other from one edition to another.

In addition to whatever additional commentary is included by the author, the typical content for a full-featured hexagram discussion will contain the following:

- King Wen's number and name for the hexagram, usually in English and Chinese, along with the Chinese pictogram for the name
- The image of the hexagram showing the different lines, along with the names for the upper and lower trigrams
- A short statement of King Wen's Decision (Judgment), which is his poetic interpretation of the hexagram's meaning and implications
- Confucius' commentary on King Wen's Decision
- Confucius' commentary on the Symbol (Image), which is a discussion on the meaning of the upper and lower trigrams
- The Yao (Line) text, which is the Duke of Zhou's poetic interpretation of the meaning of each of the six lines of the hexagram, starting with the bottom one first
- A Confucian commentary on the Duke of Zhou text

The heavy emphasis on the meaning of the individual lines of the hexagram reinforces the distinctly divinatory nature of traditional I-Ching interpretation.

# The Visionary I-Ching

While there may in fact be divinatory qualities to certain kinds of visionary experiences, either due to the recurrent nature of the life being lived by the monadic-soul or the witnessing by the monadic-soul of the experience of a future life that happens to share the same historical time frame, that is not the focus of this study's approach to hexagram exegesis. Instead, the project of matching a hexagram to a particular vision is directed at understanding the contribution of that vision to the soul's process of liberation, as measured by the amount of activation it provides to the etheric body's gateways to other lives and worlds.

Accordingly, my presentation for each hexagram will include a distinctly different set of materials than the traditional approach. The major difference with traditional treatments will be my decision to replace Duke of Zhou's account of the situation pointed to by King Wen's name for the hexagram, which he presents in six stages, with each stage matching a line of the hexagram. In its place I will describe the vision that I believe best exemplifies the essence of the hexagram. I will continue the practice of presenting it in six stages, though I do not associate any correspondence between a given line and stage. I will include two pages, one for the hexagram interpretation and the other for the vision.

The following are the major elements on the hexagram interpretation page:

- King Wen's number and name for the hexagram, usually in English and Chinese, along with the Chinese pictogram for the name
- An analysis of the meaning of the pictogram's elements, along with a reference to Wieger's *Chinese Characters*, if available (Mathews, 1996; MDBG, 2017; Wengu, 2017; Wieger, 1965)
- The image of the hexagram showing the different lines, along with the names for the upper and lower trigrams and an interpretation of the hexagram based on the meanings of the two trigrams
- A set of qualities associated with the hexagram and trigrams

- The identity of the hexagram's inner root gua and a subset of information about it, including its name and number, its two trigrams and associated meaning, and its Power Score and quartile
- For both the hexagram and its root gua, an analysis of the Yin or Yang qualities of their trigrams and which of the Four Symbols will result for each
- The Power Scoring Matrix for the hexagram, a listing of the contributions of each criterion to the total, and the total Power Score and quartile
- Finally, the total Dual Power Score formed by adding the hexagram and root gua power scores together

The following are the elements included for the hexagram vision page:

- The associated hexagram number, English and Chinese name and pictogram
- The name of the narrative to which the vision belongs
- A set of pyramids "Δ" indicating the quartile of the hexagram's total Dual Power Score: 1st quartile = "Δ Δ Δ Δ"; 2nd quartile = "Δ Δ Δ"; 3rd quartile = "Δ Δ"; and 4th quartile = "Δ"
- The number of the vision's place in the complete listing of the sixty-four vision sequence
- The name of the vision, followed by the identity of the experiencing subject of the vision
- The Activation Power Score for the vision's hexagram
- The trigram based interpretation for the hexagram, followed by the same for its root gua
- The description of the vision, presented in six stages

# Key for Hexagram Interpretation Page

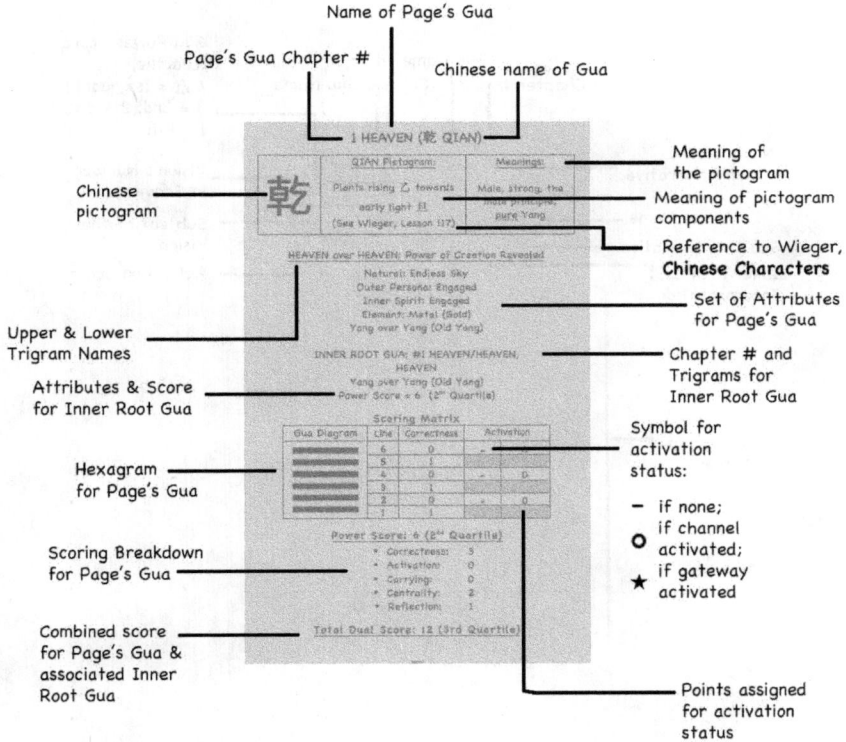

Name of Page's Gua

Page's Gua Chapter #

Chinese name of Gua

Chinese pictogram

Meaning of the pictogram

Meaning of pictogram components

Reference to Wieger, **Chinese Characters**

Set of Attributes for Page's Gua

Upper & Lower Trigram Names

Chapter # and Trigrams for Inner Root Gua

Attributes & Score for Inner Root Gua

Symbol for activation status:

Hexagram for Page's Gua

– if none;
o if channel activated;
★ if gateway activated

Scoring Breakdown for Page's Gua

Combined score for Page's Gua & associated Inner Root Gua

Points assigned for activation status

---

### 1 HEAVEN (乾 QIAN)

| QIAN Pictogram: | Meanings: |
|---|---|
| 乾 | Plants rising 乙 towards early light 日 (See Wieger, Lesson 117) | Male, strong, the male principle, pure Yang |

HEAVEN over HEAVEN: Power of Creation Revealed

Natural: Endless Sky
Outer Persona: Engaged
Inner Spirit: Engaged
Element: Metal (Gold)
Yang over Yang (Old Yang)

INNER ROOT GUA: #1 HEAVEN/HEAVEN, HEAVEN
Yang over Yang (Old Yang)
Power Score = 6 (2ⁿᵈ Quartile)

#### Scoring Matrix

| Gua Diagram | Line | Correctness | Activation |
|---|---|---|---|
| | 6 | 0 | – |
| | 5 | 1 | |
| | 4 | 0 | o |
| | 3 | 1 | |
| | 2 | 0 | o |
| | 1 | 1 | |

Power Score: 6 (2ⁿᵈ Quartile)
* Correctness: 3
* Activation: 0
* Carrying: 0
* Centrality: 2
* Reflection: 1

Total Dual Score: 12 (3rd Quartile)

62

# Key for Hexagram Vision Page

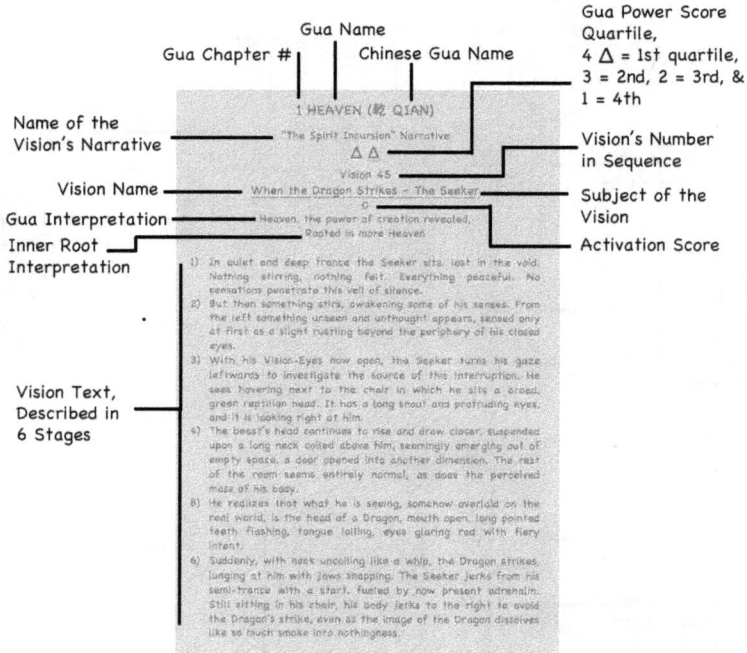

Gua Name

Gua Chapter #

Chinese Gua Name

Gua Power Score Quartile,
4 △ = 1st quartile,
3 = 2nd, 2 = 3rd, &
1 = 4th

Name of the Vision's Narrative

Vision's Number in Sequence

Vision Name

Subject of the Vision

Gua Interpretation

Inner Root Interpretation

Activation Score

Vision Text, Described in 6 Stages

---

1 HEAVEN (乾 QIAN)

"The Spirit Incursion" Narrative

△ △

Vision 45

When the Dragon Strikes - The Seeker

Heaven, the power of creation revealed.
Rooted in more Heaven.

1) In quiet and deep trance the Seeker sits, lost in the void. Nothing stirring, nothing felt. Everything peaceful. No sensations penetrate this veil of silence.

2) But then something stirs, awakening some of his senses. From the left something unseen and unthought appears, sensed only at first as a slight rustling beyond the periphery of his closed eyes.

3) With his Vision-Eyes now open, the Seeker turns his gaze leftwards to investigate the source of this interruption. He sees hovering next to the chair in which he sits a broad, green reptilian head. It has a long snout and protruding eyes, and it is looking right at him.

4) The beast's head continues to rise and draw closer, suspended upon a long neck coiled above him, seemingly emerging out of empty space, a door opened into another dimension. The rest of the room seems entirely normal, as does the perceived rest of his body.

5) He realizes that what he is seeing, somehow overlaid on the real world, is the head of a Dragon, mouth open, long pointed teeth flashing, tongue lolling, eyes glaring red with fiery intent.

6) Suddenly, with neck uncoiling like a whip, the Dragon strikes, lunging at him with jaws snapping. The Seeker jerks from his semi-trance with a start, fueled by now present adrenalin. Still sitting in his chair, his body jerks to the right to avoid the Dragon's strike, even as the image of the Dragon dissolves like so much smoke into nothingness.

## Major Subjects and Personas within the Visions

The following are either the subjects through whose eyes the visions were experienced or other major characters found within the visions:

- *The Seeker*: the author when present in the mundane world and during the initial stages of meditation
- *The Witness*: the author involved in a vision only as a passive, non-embodied observer and not engaged within the vision as a participant
- *The Traveller*: the author as an active participant in the vision as a version of himself, usually as a 35-year old. Also the general name for the author's persona in his visionary odyssey. Note the two "l's" to indicate the special kind of travel involved
- *The Rider*: the author when he occupies the body of a non-human entity who is a participant within the vision, such as the Dragon
- *The Other-Self*: the character of the author seen in a vision while sitting in meditation as the Seeker
- *The Teacher*: the wise woman who guides and instructs the Traveller in his journey's through the visions
- *The First Son*: the first born, teenage son of his jungle tribe's chief (his father) and queen shaman (his mother)
- *The Spirit Walker*: the ceremonial name for First Son's mother, the tribe's shaman, who possesses psychic powers
- *The Apprentice Blacksmith*: the young, peasant apprentice who is a member of the Watchers, who serve as lookouts for their village, and is conscripted into the King's service
- *The King*: the ruler of the castle that includes the apprentice's village in its domain
- *The Shadow Warrior*: the champion of the Dark Army that is arrayed against the King and whom the apprentice must challenge
- *The Adept*: one of a series of cloned youths who are in training to be elevated into the Dragon Clan and prepared for entry into the sacred Pyramid
- *The Journeyman*: the Adept, newly elevated, who, having passed selection rituals, has been granted entrance into the Pyramid
- *The Magister*: the head of the Council of Elders who awaits the Traveller's completion of his journey and readiness for further advancement

# The Visionary I-Ching: 64 Gua & Visions

# 1 HEAVEN (乾 QIAN)

| 乾 | QIAN Pictogram:<br><br>Plants rising 乙 towards<br><br>early light 旦<br>(See Wieger, Lesson 117) | Meanings:<br><br>Male, strong, the male principle;<br>Pure Yang |
|---|---|---|

### HEAVEN over HEAVEN: Power of Creation Revealed

Natural: Endless Sky
Outer Persona: Engaged
Inner Spirit: Engaged
Element: Metal (Gold)
Yang over Yang (Old Yang)

INNER ROOT GUA: #1 HEAVEN/HEAVEN,
HEAVEN
Yang over Yang (Old Yang)
Power Score = 6  (2nd Quartile)

### Scoring Matrix

| Gua Diagram | Line | Correctness | Activation | |
|---|---|---|---|---|
| | 6 | 0 | – | 0 |
| | 5 | 1 | | |
| | 4 | 0 | – | 0 |
| | 3 | 1 | | |
| | 2 | 0 | – | 0 |
| | 1 | 1 | | |

## Power Score: 6 (2nd Quartile)

- Correctness: 3
- Activation: 0
- Carrying: 0
- Centrality: 2
- Reflection: 1

## Total Dual Score: 12 (3rd Quartile)

# 1 HEAVEN (乾 QIAN)

"The Spirit Incursion" Narrative

Δ Δ

## Vision 45
### When the Dragon Strikes – The Seeker
O
Heaven, the power of creation revealed,
Rooted in more Heaven

1) In quiet and deep trance the Seeker sits, lost in the void. Nothing stirring, nothing felt. Everything peaceful. No sensations penetrate this veil of silence.
2) But then something stirs, awakening some of his senses. From the left something unseen and unthought appears, sensed only at first as a slight rustling beyond the periphery of his closed eyes.
3) With his Vision-Eyes now open, the Seeker turns his gaze leftwards to investigate the source of this interruption. He sees hovering next to the chair in which he sits a broad, green reptilian head. It has a long snout and protruding eyes, and it is looking right at him.
4) The beast's head continues to rise and draw closer, suspended upon a long neck coiled above him, seemingly emerging out of empty space, a door opened into another dimension. The rest of the room seems entirely normal, as does the perceived mass of his body.
5) He realizes that what he is seeing, somehow overlaid on the real world, is the head of a Dragon, mouth open, long pointed teeth flashing, tongue lolling, eyes glaring red with fiery intent.
6) Suddenly, with neck uncoiling like a whip, the Dragon strikes, lunging at him with jaws snapping. The Seeker jerks from his semi-trance with a start, fueled by now present adrenalin. Still sitting in his chair, his body jerks to the right to avoid the Dragon's strike, even as the image of the Dragon dissolves like so much smoke into nothingness.

## 2 EARTH (坤 KUN)

| 坤 | KUN Pictogram:<br><br>Soil 土 from which all<br><br>things extend 申 | Meanings:<br><br>The earth,<br>female principle;<br>Pure Yin |
|---|---|---|

**EARTH over EARTH: Nurtured in Receptive Fields**

Natural: Open Plains
Outer Persona: Yielding
Inner Spirit: Yielding
Element: Earth
Yin over Yin (Old Yin)

INNER ROOT GUA: #2 EARTH/EARTH,
EARTH
Yin over Yin (Old Yin)
Power Score = 4 (3$^{rd}$ Quartile)

### Scoring Matrix

| Gua Diagram | Line | Correctness | Activation | |
|---|---|---|---|---|
| | 6 | 1 | - | 0 |
| | 5 | 0 | | |
| | 4 | 1 | - | 0 |
| | 3 | 0 | | |
| | 2 | 1 | - | 0 |
| | 1 | 0 | | |

## Power Score: 4 (3$^{rd}$ Quartile)

- Correctness: 3
- Activation: 0
- Carrying: 0
- Centrality: 0
- Reflection: 1

## Total Dual Score: 8 (4$^{th}$ Quartile)

## 2 EARTH (坤 KUN)

"The Spirit Incursion" Narrative

Δ

## Vision 39
### The Descent of Power – The Seeker
O
Earth, nurtured in receptive fields,
Rooted in more Earth

1) From deep trance the Seeker lurches awake to discover his heart racing and breath panting. His eyes spring open. He is in his room, sitting in his meditation chair, as expected. But all is not normal.

2) The room itself is shaking. Quiet ambient meditation music had been playing on a portable CD player set on the floor in the corner of the room to his left. It is quiet no more. The CD is now emphatically stuck in a repeating loop, rapidly skipping back and forth, like a defective vinyl record. The sound is so loud and cacophonous that the Seeker is unable to form any thoughts about what is happening.

3) The crown of the Seeker's head feels as if it has been pried open, with flowing, electric energy rushing down his spine. A completely new, unexpected sensation, it continues to overload his capacity for reflective thought.

4) This fiery energy spirals unabated down his back, penetrating to the base of his spine, where it collects in an expanding pool of vibrating, liquid heat.

5) The flow keeps coming and coming until the Seeker can take no more, his ability to absorb any additional energy lost, his reservoir full. He feels like he is vibrating all over, as the accumulated power pushes to escape its bodily confinement.

6) Shaking, he feels trapped in its grace and power, his Self lost in the depths of its ecstasy.

## 3 SPROUTING (屯 ZHUN)

| | ZHUN Pictogram: | Meanings: |
|---|---|---|
| 屯 | The young plant struggling to rise to the surface (See Wieger, Lesson 79) | Difficult, to station (soldiers), to store up |

### WATER over THUNDER: The Immersed Rising

Natural: Rain falls on emerging Life
Outer Persona: Immersed
Inner Spirit: Aroused
Element: Water
Yin over Yang (Young Yin)

INNER ROOT GUA: #36 EARTH/FIRE,
CONCEALED BRILLIANCE
Yin over Yang (Young Yin)
Power Score = 9 (1st Quartile)

### Scoring Matrix

| Gua Diagram | Line | Correctness | Activation | |
|---|---|---|---|---|
| | 6 | 1 | O | 1 |
| | 5 | 1 | | |
| | 4 | 1 | O | 1 |
| | 3 | 0 | | |
| | 2 | 1 | ★ | 2 |
| | 1 | 1 | | |

### Power Score: 12 (1st Quartile)

- Correctness: 5
- Activation: 4
- Carrying: 1
- Centrality: 2
- Reflection: 0

### Total Dual Score: 21 (1st Quartile)

## 3 SPROUTING (屯 ZHUN)

"The Heavenly Revelation" Narrative

△ △ △ △

Vision 58

### The Yellow Sprout – The Seeker

4

Sprouting, with the immersed rising,
Rooted in Concealed Brilliance

1) Sitting in shallow trance, the Seeker sees floating before him a patch of barren yellow brown dirt, looking like recent rains have moistened it. He feels himself simultaneously sitting in the chair and hovering above this ground.

2) Everything is quiet and still. As of yet, nothing has grown on this ground. Only small rocks and gravel litter its surface. No life of any kind is visible.

3) Suddenly something begins to stir in the center of this empty region, rising from below and displacing small pieces of earth and gravel, a small eruption of activity.

4) A yellow shoot breaks through its earthen ceiling, turning and undulating, this way and that, as if it were looking around to assess its surroundings.

5) It continues to emerge, snake-like in its appearance and gyrations, wiggling its way out of the confining grip of the clinging soil. As the shoot's movements slow, he gets the feeling that it is looking directly at him. He realizes that this sprout is not plant but a freshly hatched wyrmling, newly emerged into the air.

6) Watching this scene, the Seeker senses a change in the atmosphere, as if some unknown presence had suddenly appeared. Within his mind he hears a voice. "Do not go to heaven." As the vision fades away and he returns to normal consciousness, he is left puzzled and somewhat angered by this utterance.

# 4 CHILDHOOD (蒙 MENG)

| 蒙 | MENG Pictogram:<br><br>Plant ⁺⁺ that covers 冢<br>(See Wieger, Lesson 34) | Meanings:<br><br>Cover, deceive, cheat |
|---|---|---|

## MOUNTAIN over WATER: Binding the Darkness

Natural: Streams flow in Mountain Valley
Outer Persona: Stubborn
Inner Spirit: Immersed
Element: Earth
Yang over Yin (Young Yang)

INNER ROOT GUA: #35 FIRE/EARTH,
PROGRESS
Yang over Yin (Young Yang)
Power Score = 1 (4th Quartile)

### Scoring Matrix

| Gua Diagram | Line | Correctness | Activation | |
|---|---|---|---|---|
| | 6 | 0 | – | 0 |
| | 5 | 0 | | |
| | 4 | 1 | – | 0 |
| | 3 | 0 | | |
| | 2 | 0 | – | 0 |
| | 1 | 0 | | |

## Power Score: 2 (4th Quartile)

- Correctness: 1
- Activation: 0
- Carrying: 0
- Centrality: 1
- Reflection: 0

## Total Dual Score: 3 (4ᵗʰ Quartile)

# 4 CHILDHOOD (蒙 MENG)

"The Pyramid Ascension" Narrative

Δ

## Vision 23
### The Valley of the Solitary Oaks -- The Witness
O

Childhood, binding the darkness,
Rooted in Progress

1) Rising up through dark waters, the Witness hovers above a blue river meandering through a verdant mountain valley, brightly lit by sunlight in a cloud sprinkled sky.
2) Ranges of blue grey mountains fade into the distance. They surround a series of small rolling hills, each crowned with a single majestic oak tree and nothing else. The greens of the valley are saturated, glowing with the fresh growth of new spring. The Witness gets the impression that he is inside a pastoral landscape painting.
3) The Witness' view quickly moves from hill to hill and from tree to tree, growing ever closer to the surrounding peaks, not knowing what is driving his movements.
4) He stops at a hill where he sees the Teacher perched before the hill's tree. She approaches the tree and peels back the bark from its wide trunk, revealing a hidden, arched shaped area built in the tree.
5) Some kind of apparatus is contained there. Manipulating an unseen mechanism, she folds down a chair connected to the tree. She sits on it, her back to the tree, facing a nearby mountain range.
6) Suddenly the Witness' gaze is pulled away from the seated Teacher and rapidly propelled into the air, flying up the side of the highest visible mountain slope. He sees only blue sky and clouds rushing at him.

# 5 WAITING (需 XU)

| 需 | XU Pictogram:<br>Rains 雨 necessary for small<br>plants 而 to take root<br>(See Wieger, Lesson 164) | Meanings:<br><br>To require,<br>need |
|---|---|---|

## WATER over HEAVEN: Immersed Power

Natural: Rain clouds in the Sky
Outer Persona: Immersed
Inner Spirit: Engaged
Element: Water
Yin over Yang (Young Yin)

## INNER ROOT GUA: #34 THUNDER/HEAVEN, GREAT STRENGTH
Yang over Yang (Old Yang)
Power Score = 5 (3rd Quartile)

### Scoring Matrix

| Gua Diagram | Line | Correctness | Activation | |
|---|---|---|---|---|
| | 6 | 1 | ★ | 2 |
| | 5 | 1 | | |
| | 4 | 1 | ★ | 2 |
| | 3 | 1 | | |
| | 2 | 0 | – | 0 |
| | 1 | 1 | | |

## Power Score: 12 (1st Quartile)
- Correctness: 5
- Activation: 4
- Carrying: 1
- Centrality: 2
- Reflection: 0

## Total Dual Score: 17 (1st Quartile)

# 5 WAITING (需 XU)

"The Dragon Encounter" Narrative

△ △ △ △

Vision 12

## The Dragon in the Swamp – The First Son

4

Waiting, with immersed power,
Rooted in Great Strength

1) First Son and his young friends stand at the edge of the swamp, waiting to catch a glimpse of an old crocodile rumored to have come to their jungle. They are on a hunting trail, surrounded on each side by thick tropical jungle growth and towering trees.

2) Scanning the water's edge, they spy two red eyes peering at them from the swamp. Soon thereafter, the rest of a green reptilian head emerges, glaring hungrily at them, its girth larger than expected, its tongue flicking.

3) First Son reaches for a stone to throw at what he thinks is the old crocodile, wanting to show off for his friends, but a sudden feeling in his gut freezes him and sends him hastily retreating down the path, followed by the other children.

4) Looking over his shoulder he sees the head continuing to rise higher above the waters, visible now on top of a long, erect, sinewy neck, its back lined with pointed crests.

5) The creature crawls from the water on muscular legs atop a massive, snake-like body, violently shaking the water off. This is not a crocodile. It is the Dragon found in their tribe's campfire stories, the one their parents frighten them with when they misbehave. It is real, and it is coming for them.

6) As the children, breathless, approach the hoped for safety of their village, they are relieved to hear the frustrated roars of the Dragon receding into the distance. Traces of burnt sulfur and vegetation linger in the air. First Son sees his mother, the tribe's Spirit Walker, angrily waiting for him with crossed arms. She doesn't look happy.

# 6 CONTENTION (訟 SONG)

| 訟 | SONG Pictogram:<br><br>Words 言 for the public 厷 | Meanings:<br><br>Litigation |
|---|---|---|

### HEAVEN over WATER: Power of Darkness

Natural: Rain pours from Sky
Outer Persona: Engaged
Inner Spirit: Immersed
Element: Metal (Gold)
Yang over Yin (Young Yang)

INNER ROOT GUA: #33 HEAVEN/MOUNTAIN,
RETREAT
Yin over Yang (Young Yin)
Power Score = 6 (2nd Quartile)

## Scoring Matrix

| Gua Diagram | Line | Correctness | Activation | |
|---|---|---|---|---|
| | 6 | 0 | - | 0 |
| | 5 | 1 | | |
| | 4 | 0 | - | 0 |
| | 3 | 0 | | |
| | 2 | 0 | - | 0 |
| | 1 | 0 | | |

## Power Score: 3 (4th Quartile)

- Correctness: 1
- Activation: 0
- Carrying: 0
- Centrality: 2
- Reflection: 0

## Total Dual Score: 9 (3rd Quartile)

# 6 CONTENTION (訟 SONG)

"The Castle Redemption" Narrative

Δ Δ

## Vision 27

### The Shadow Warrior – The Apprentice Smith

O

Contention, with power of darkness,
Rooted in Retreat

1) Sent alone from the castle to face the Dark Army's champion, the Apprentice Blacksmith carries no weapon. For armor he wears only ill-fitting rusted chainmail and a torn, soiled tunic, secured with a rope for a belt.

2) There the Shadow Warrior waits, massive, standing over 7 feet tall, his impassive face broad and features coarse. He is fitted with black leather armor and leggings, covered with silver spikes and studs. Even at a distance he towers over him.

3) The Apprentice hesitantly walks towards the Shadow Warrior. Suddenly the Warrior lunges at him, swinging wildly, as the Apprentice frantically slips and dodges beneath his blows. He takes heart in seeing that the Shadow Warrior's movements are stiff and awkward.

4) The Shadow Warrior is too big for him to hurt with strikes. Remembering his training, the Apprentice deflects a wild left, and using its momentum to pull it across his body, sweeps the Warrior's leading leg out from under him.

5) The Shadow Warrior goes down hard, striking his head on the rocky ground, losing consciousness.

6) Black swirling vapors begin to flow from the Shadow Warrior's mouth and nose. Quickly the Apprentice crouches over him to harvest the escaping Shadow Energies, rapidly inhaling them before they could dissipate. He must get these to the King.

# 7 MULTITUDE (師 SHI)

| 師 | SHI Pictogram:<br><br>Legion 垍 that surrounds 匝<br>(See Wieger, Lesson 86) | Meanings:<br><br>A division, army, multitude |
|---|---|---|

### EARTH over WATER: Receptive to Motion

Natural: Underground Springs
Outer Persona: Yielding
Inner Spirit: Immersed
Element: Earth
Yin over Yin (Old Yin)

INNER ROOT GUA: #16 THUNDER/EARTH,
DELIGHT
Yang over Yin (Young Yang)
Power Score = 2 (4<sup>th</sup> Quartile)

### Scoring Matrix

| Gua Diagram | Line | Correctness | Activation | |
|---|---|---|---|---|
| | 6 | 1 | – | 0 |
| | 5 | 0 | | |
| | 4 | 1 | – | 0 |
| | 3 | 0 | | |
| | 2 | 0 | – | 0 |
| | 1 | 0 | | |

## Power Score: 3 (4th Quartile)

- Correctness: 2
- Activation: 0
- Carrying: 0
- Centrality: 1
- Reflection: 0

## Total Dual Score: 5 (4<sup>th</sup> Quartile)

# 7 MULTITUDE (師 SHI)

"The Pyramid Ascension" Narrative

Δ

## Vision 32
## The Village of Adepts –The Witness

O

The Multitude, receptive to motion,
Rooted in Delight

1) Next to a wide, languidly flowing river, the Witness, looking down to his right, sees a primitive village, mud huts with straw roofs scattered across open fields. In the distance he spies desert dunes and the top of what appears to be a pyramid.

2) Palm trees and lush vegetation line the riverbanks, but there is nothing growing amid the huts, the yellow sandy ground worn bare and hard packed by constant traffic.

3) Initially the village appears empty, but then, as if from a signal, individuals start pouring from the huts. From his viewpoint hovering above them, they all look similar in appearance, with brown skin and short black hair, identical in size and build. They appear Middle Eastern in nationality.

4) All appear young, maybe in their mid 20's, with no older individuals in sight. He sees no one supervising or giving them any kind of direction. They are all uniformly dressed, with loose white pants and short-sleeved white tunics. They are all barefoot.

5) Their movements appear un-choreographed, though they are all engaged in the same activity, spinning and swinging long wooden staffs, as they randomly wander among their camp, somehow avoiding each other.

6) From what he observes, the scene looks to the Traveller like some kind of impromptu martial arts training facility, with its own kind of strange balletic grace.

## 8 UNITY (比 BI)

| | BI Pictogram: | Meanings: |
|---|---|---|
| 比 | Two persons 匕 next to each other (See Wieger, Lesson 27) | Associate with, be near, to compare, to contrast |

### WATER over EARTH: Flowing Receptivity

Natural: Water flowing on the Earth
Outer Persona: Immersed
Inner Spirit: Yielding
Element: Water
Yin over Yin (Old Yin)

### INNER ROOT GUA: #15 EARTH/MOUNTAIN, HUMBLENESS
Yin over Yang (Young Yin)
Power Score = 6 (2nd Quartile)

### Scoring Matrix

| Gua Diagram | Line | Correctness | Activation | |
|---|---|---|---|---|
| | 6 | 1 | O | 1 |
| | 5 | 1 | | |
| | 4 | 1 | – | 0 |
| | 3 | 0 | | |
| | 2 | 1 | O | 1 |
| | 1 | 0 | | |

### Power Score: 9 (1st Quartile)
- Correctness: 4
- Activation: 2
- Carrying: 1
- Centrality: 2
- Reflection: 0

### Total Dual Score: 15 (2nd Quartile)

# 8 UNITY (比 BI)

"The Hidden Source" Narrative

△ △ △

Vision 16

## The Three Sisters – The Witness

2

Unity, with flowing receptivity,
Rooted in Humbleness

1) Floating in an empty void, the Witness hears several voices talking, apparently somewhere above him. He cannot make out what they are saying.

2) Looking up, he sees three separate, rectangular shaped windowed areas, floating in empty space, lined up next to each other. The boundaries between them are not sharp, but appear fuzzy and amorphous.

3) In each window the head of a different woman is visible, all having straight brown hair and facial features and all roughly the same age, being in their mid thirties.

4) All of these women are speaking, sometimes while facing each other, sometimes not, sometimes taking turns, sometimes talking all at once. Are they talking to each other? He is unsure.

5) Try as he might, he cannot make out what they are saying. Initially believing that this was some kind of strange psychic chat room, he soon realizes after further observation they are not speaking to one another but instead to some unseen party in each of their own windows.

6) The Witness has one more revelation. He realizes that not only do these three women look enough alike to be sisters, but they also each resemble the Teacher figure he has seen before. Could there be more than one Teacher?

# 9 SMALL ACCUMULATION (小畜 XIAO CHU)

| 小畜 | XIAO CHU Pictogram: Small 小 covered 玄 field 田 (farm) (See Wieger, Lesson 91) | Meanings: Small livestock collection |
|---|---|---|

### WIND over HEAVEN: Focused Power

Natural: Wings in the Sky
Outer Persona: Focused
Inner Spirit: Engaged
Element: Wood
Yin over Yang (Young Yin)

### INNER ROOT GUA: #14 FIRE/HEAVEN, GREAT HARVEST
Yang over Yang (Old Yang)
Power Score = 3 (4$^{th}$ Quartile)

## Scoring Matrix

| Gua Diagram | Line | Correctness | Activation | |
|---|---|---|---|---|
| | 6 | 0 | – | 0 |
| | 5 | 1 | | |
| | 4 | 1 | ★ | 2 |
| | 3 | 1 | | |
| | 2 | 0 | – | 0 |
| | 1 | 1 | | |

## Power Score: 9 (1st Quartile)

- Correctness: 4
- Activation: 2
- Carrying: 1
- Centrality: 2
- Reflection: 0

## Total Dual Score: 12 (3rd Quartile)

# 9 SMALL ACCUMULATION (小畜 XIAO CHU)

### "The Castle Redemption" Narrative

## △ △

### Vision 24
### The Dragon Watch – The Apprentice Smith
2
Small Accumulation, with focused power,
Rooted in Great Harvest

1) The Apprentice Blacksmith stands on the leveled edge of a mountain outlook on a wooden platform. He is buffeted by high winds, as he gazes below right into a river valley formed by cascading rows of mountains receding into the distance. This valley looks familiar to him, and he is trying to pick out familiar landmarks.

2) He is not alone on this outcrop, for there are several others standing behind him, talking and joking with one another.

3) Still staring down into the valley, he is jostled by someone behind him, who tells him to do his job and watch the sky.

4) He reminds himself why he is there. He is not a sightseer, but part of a group of Watchers, whose job it is to scan the skies above for signs of danger.

5) Of course, as always, he is bored and restless, since nothing ever happens. He sees in the distance a dark flying shape. Probably just another large bird, he thinks to himself, maybe an eagle, looking to prey on the village's small animals.

6) The shape gets larger and larger the closer it gets. As its features become clearer he realizes with a start that it is not a bird. It has enormous angular wings and a long body and neck. It is the Sky Dragon, and it is in search of larger prey. The Watchers sound the alarm and rush back to warn the village.

## 10 TREADING (履 LU)

| 履 | LU Pictogram:<br><br>Body 尸 repeating 复<br><br>steps 彳 (See Wieger, Lesson 75) | Meanings:<br><br>Shoes, to<br>tread on |
|---|---|---|

### HEAVEN over LAKE: Powerful Passion

Natural: Sky over a Lake
Outer Persona: Engaged
Inner Spirit: Passionate
Element: Metal (Gold)
Yang over Yin (Young Yang)

INNER ROOT GUA: #13 HEAVEN/FIRE,
SEEKING HARMONY
Yang over Yang (Old Yang)
Power Score = 8 (2$^{nd}$ Quartile)

### Scoring Matrix

| Gua Diagram | Line | Correctness | Activation | |
|---|---|---|---|---|
| | 6 | 0 | – | 0 |
| | 5 | 1 | | |
| | 4 | 0 | – | 0 |
| | 3 | 0 | | |
| | 2 | 0 | – | 0 |
| | 1 | 1 | | |

### Power Score: 4 (3$^{rd}$ Quartile)

- Correctness: 2
- Activation: 0
- Carrying: 0
- Centrality: 2
- Reflection: 0

### Total Dual Score: 12 (3$^{rd}$ Quartile)

# 10 TREADING (履 LU)

"The Pyramid Ascension" Narrative

△ △

## Vision 35
## The Golden Corridor – The Journeyman
O
Treading, with powerful passion,
Rooted in Seeking Harmony

1) The Journeyman walks through the narrow, dark, tunnels of the ancient pyramid. The corridors are hewn out of rough rock, squarish in shape.
2) Other similarly attired individuals accompany him. All, like him, are wearing khaki pants and vests over loosely fitting white shirts. He alone wears a broad rimmed safari hat.
3) The tunnel narrows further until rounding a corner it suddenly becomes wider. Its formerly downward slope now begins to curve upwards. The walls, no longer square, become much more rounded.
4) The walls and floors are now smooth and metallic, more like the rounded corridors of a vessel than a passage through a rocky mound. The corridor curves upwards sharply to the left.
5) Looking at the inside wall, a golden sphere of light follows his gaze. The wall, crafted out of solid gold, is not bare, but covered with row after row of engraved hieroglyphs and symbols, a strange blend of Egyptian, Hebrew, Chinese and Greek markings.
6) A bright white glow emanates from the unseen area around the corner. The curved gold walls abruptly end, replaced by a chamber with white walls. He hears machinelike sounds of humming.

# 11 ADVANCE (泰 TAI)

| 泰 | TAI Pictogram:<br><br>Water 水 running through<br>person's 大 hands 廾<br>(See Wieger, Lesson 47) | Meanings:<br><br>Safe, peaceful, prosperous |
|---|---|---|

EARTH over HEAVEN: Yielding to Power

Natural: High plateaus
Outer Persona: Yielding
Inner Spirit: Engaged
Element: Earth
Yin over Yang (Young Yin)

INNER ROOT GUA: #54 THUNDER/LAKE,
DOMESTICATED MAIDEN
Power Score = 3 (4<sup>th</sup> Quartile)
Yang over Yin (Young Yang)

## Scoring Matrix

| Gua Diagram | Line | Correctness | Activation | |
|---|---|---|---|---|
| | 6 | 1 | O | 1 |
| | 5 | 0 | | |
| | 4 | 1 | ★ | 2 |
| | 3 | 1 | | |
| | 2 | 0 | – | 0 |
| | 1 | 1 | | |

## Power Score: 8 (2<sup>nd</sup> Quartile)

- Correctness: 4
- Activation: 3
- Carrying: 0
- Centrality: 1
- Reflection: 0

## Total Dual Score: 11 (3<sup>rd</sup> Quartile)

# 11 ADVANCE (泰 TAI)

## "The Heavenly Revelation" Narrative

## △ △

## Vision 59

### Behind the Blue Door – The Seeker

3

Advance, yielding to power,
Rooted in the Domesticated Maiden

1) The Seeker, in trance, sits in the chair in his room, his Vision-Eyes open.

2) Before him, he sees the familiar bookshelf and other elements lining the front wall, with the room's door to the right, as expected.

3) Suddenly he sees floating at eye level in front of the bookshelf a blue robed, younger version of himself, hair dark and long, face unlined, sitting in full lotus position, with eyes closed. The figure of the Other-Self is clearly deep in a meditative trance.

4) The eyes of the floating figure open and look directly at him. Suddenly the Seeker is now seeing through the Other-Self's eyes, looking back at the now empty chair where he formerly sat.

5) The scene continues to change. The window, which overlooked the pond in the backyard and was set in the wall directly behind and above the chair, has vanished. The wall is solid and now a stark shade of white.

6) Where before there was a blank wall, a door has suddenly appeared. The chair also is gone. The door is solid and unmarked, painted a rich cobalt blue with a silver colored doorknob. The knob begins to turn and the door slowly opens, revealing a glimpse of a lit space behind the wall.

## 12 HINDRANCE (否 PI)

| 否 | PI Pictogram:<br><br>Mouth 口 saying no 不 (a bird flying away) (See Wieger, Lesson 133) | Meanings:<br><br>To negate, to deny, clogged, evil |
|---|---|---|

### HEAVEN over EARTH: Power Yielding

Natural: Sky dwarfing the Land
Outer Persona: Engaged
Inner Spirit: Yielding
Element: Metal (Gold)
Yang over Yin (Young Yang)

INNER ROOT GUA: #53 WIND/MOUNTAIN,
DEVELOP GRADUALLY
Yin over Yang (Young Yin)
Power Score = 9 (1$^{st}$ Quartile)

### Scoring Matrix

| Gua Diagram | Line | Correctness | Activation | |
|---|---|---|---|---|
| | 6 | 0 | – | 0 |
| | 5 | 1 | | |
| | 4 | 0 | – | 0 |
| | 3 | 0 | | |
| | 2 | 1 | O | 1 |
| | 1 | 0 | | |

## Power Score: 5 (3$^{rd}$ Quartile)

- Correctness: 2
- Activation: 1
- Carrying: 0
- Centrality: 2
- Reflection: 0

## Total Dual Score: 14 (2$^{nd}$ Quartile)

## 12 HINDRANCE (否 PI)

"The Hidden Source" Narrative

△ △ △

### Vision 21
### White Light Blocked – The Seeker
1

Hindrance, with power yielding,
Rooted in Gradual Development

1) The Seeker, floating in trance, sees a solid white void. It lacks any texture or variation of light or shadow, more like a smooth sheet of blank paper than an open navigable expanse.

2) Though hovering in place, the Seeker feels himself separated from this empty whiteness, as if it were a solid object for his perusal. At this point there is no impression of depth, only flatness.

3) This sense of flatness disappears as the Seeker starts to slowly drift towards the upper right corner of the empty tableau. He is now inside the whiteness, being pulled into its depths.

4) A vortex-like disturbance forms in the area to which he is being drawn. Small at first, the vibrating distortion begins to grow in size and intensity, as does the magnitude of the pulling force. A line from an old movie come to him, "Do not go into the light."

5) This area is now like a white broiling sun, with light blinding in its intensity. He is being drawn closer and closer to this turbulent white fire, like a fish being pulled out of its dark watery depths into blinding sunlight.

6) Suddenly, like a gate slamming shut, three black horizontal bars materialize across the center of his visual field, obscuring the boiling vortex. Shadowy rays of light stream through the bars from the anomaly, but enough of its gravitational force has been disrupted to stop his forward progress. Once again he floats in place, bathed now in streams of soft white light.

## 13 SEEKING HARMONY (同人 TONG REN)

| 同人 | Tong Ren Pictogram: People 人 brought together 同 (See Wieger, Lesson 34) | Meanings: Togetherness, fellowship, kindred |
|---|---|---|

### HEAVEN over FIRE: Power of Illumination

Natural: Lightning strikes downward
Outer Persona: Engaged
Inner Spirit: Excited
Element: Metal (Gold)
Yang over Yang (Old Yang)

INNER ROOT GUA: #9 WIND/HEAVEN,
SMALL ACCUMULATION
Yin over Yang (Young Yin)
Power Score = 9 (1st Quartile)

### Scoring Matrix

| Gua Diagram | Line | Correctness | Activation | |
|---|---|---|---|---|
| | 6 | 0 | – | 0 |
| | 5 | 1 | | |
| | 4 | 0 | – | 0 |
| | 3 | 1 | | |
| | 2 | 1 | ★ | 2 |
| | 1 | 1 | | |

### Power Score: 8 (2nd Quartile)

- Correctness: 4
- Activation: 2
- Carrying: 0
- Centrality: 2
- Reflection: 0

### Total Dual Score: 17 (1st Quartile)

# 13 SEEKING HARMONY (同人 TONG REN)

"The Face of the Deep" Narrative
## △ △ △ △
## Vision 9
## Golden Light Reflections – The Seeker
2
Seeking Harmony, with power of illumination,
Rooted in Small Accumulation

1) The Seeker, sitting in trance, sees a colorless, empty expanse, neither black nor white. Soon, a perfectly square window begins to take shape in the center of his vision. He sees only the square. The space around it is now invisible.

2) Within the window, a brightly colored field of azure blue appears. The image is not that of an unmoving, solid shape, however, but more like the fluid-like surface of a watery volume.

3) Horizontal rows of waves cover the field's surface. Each row is made up of a series of repeating segments of identical, polygonally shaped facets, like so many diamond shaped teeth. He recognizes these shapes as the result of some kind of wind-blown choppiness.

4) As the image comes into further focus, it begins to move. The waves with their pyramid shaped clusters of chop slowly undulate across the watery surface, flowing from the bottom of the image to the top, at a gradual, constant pace.

5) At the diamond shaped tip of each of the choppy wave segments, a bright golden light glistens and sparkles, reflections from an unseen sun in the skies above it.

6) After a short interval, the blue background begins to get darker and darker, going from blue to purple to black. Soon, all that remains is a field of sparkling golden stars in a black night sky.

## 14 GREAT HARVEST (大有 DA YOU)

| 大有 | Da You Pictogram: Great 大 having 有 (hand grabbing the moon) (See Wieger, Lesson 46) | Meanings: Great possession |
|---|---|---|

### FIRE over HEAVEN: Clinging Power

Natural: Lightning across the Sky
Outer Persona: Excited
Inner Spirit: Engaged
Element: Fire
Yang over Yang (Old Yang)

### INNER ROOT GUA: #10 HEAVEN/LAKE, TREADING
Yang over Yin (Young Yang)
Power Score = 4 (3rd Quartile)

### Scoring Matrix

| Gua Diagram | Line | Correctness | Activation | |
|---|---|---|---|---|
| | 6 | 0 | – | 0 |
| | 5 | 0 | | |
| | 4 | 0 | – | 0 |
| | 3 | 1 | | |
| | 2 | 0 | – | 0 |
| | 1 | 1 | | |

### Power Score: 3 (4th Quartile)

- Correctness:  2
- Activation:  0
- Carrying:  0
- Centrality:  1
- Reflection:  0

### Total Dual Score: 7 (4th Quartile)

# 14 GREAT HARVEST (大有 DA YOU)

"The Nexus Formation" Narrative

Δ

## Vision 5
### The Spirit Migration – The Traveller
O
Great Harvest, with clinging power,
Rooted in Treading

1) The Traveller is walking through a redwood and oak forest along a dirt-covered hiking trail.
2) The trail is set in a small depression next to an upward sloping hillside on the left and a downward slope on the right. Trees line both sides, which is thick with brush and grasses and ferns.
3) The walk proceeds uneventfully until he perceives what feels like a shift in atmospheric pressure. The leaves of the trees and the grasses and ferns begin to rustle, even though there is no apparent wind.
4) At this moment he is engulfed on all sides by a sea of small, translucence, glistening objects floating upwards into the sky. He looks for their place of origin but finds none. They are not coming out of the ground, but rather seem to be just materializing out of thin air, already in motion.
5) These objects are about the size and shape of a hand with fingers cupped together, pointed upwards, like an upside down jellyfish. Like a jellyfish, they have a pearly, incandescent, shimmering color to them, lit by glowing, internal, luminous phosphorescence.
6) They shimmer like thousands of sparkling flames as they rise into the air, row after row ascending in a seemingly endless progression into the heavens.

# 15 HUMBLENESS (謙 QIAN)

| 謙 | QIAN Pictogram:<br><br>Words 言 uniting 兼<br>(See Wieger, Lesson 73, 44) | Meanings:<br><br>Modest, humble |
|---|---|---|

**EARTH over MOUNTAIN: Receptive to Stillness**

Natural: Alpine meadows
Outer Persona: Yielding
Inner Spirit: Stubborn
Element: Earth
Yin over Yang (Young Yin)

INNER ROOT GUA: #7 EARTH/WATER,
MULTITUDE
Yang over Yin (Young Yang)
Power Score = 3 (4$^{th}$ Quartile)

## Scoring Matrix

| Gua Diagram | Line | Correctness | Activation | |
|---|---|---|---|---|
| | 6 | 1 | O | 1 |
| | 5 | 0 | | |
| | 4 | 1 | O | 1 |
| | 3 | 1 | | |
| | 2 | 1 | – | 0 |
| | 1 | 0 | | |

## Power Score: 6 (2$^{nd}$ Quartile)

- Correctness: 4
- Activation: 2
- Carrying: 0
- Centrality: 0
- Reflection: 0

## Total Dual Score: 9 (3$^{rd}$ Quartile)

# 15 HUMBLENESS (謙 QIAN)

"The Dragon Encounter" Narrative

Δ Δ

## Vision 15
### Choosing the Mystic Path – The Seeker
2

Humbleness, receptive to stillness,
Rooted in Multitude

1) The Seeker, sitting in a trance, sees images of two adjacent caves. The caves are set into the sides of a cliff. Each cave occupies half his visual field. A fuzzy, amorphous border separates them, as if he were looking through binoculars, with each cave appearing in a distinct eyepiece.

2) At the front of each cave he sees a similar sight: a man sitting in a relaxed cross-legged lotus position, eyes closed, lost in meditation. Each is a grizzled looking, 50ish years old, Eastern European man. Both are dressed similarly, in dark clothes wearing a loose overcoat and a "peasant" cap.

3) The only real difference in the apparel of the two is that the man on the left wears brown clothes and the man on the right blue grey clothes. Their appearance is so similar that they might be brothers or even fraternal twins.

4) He has the distinct impression that in spite of the obvious similarities, these are two distinct individuals from different time frames who both happen to be mystics.

5) He also considers that each of these men might be himself in a previous incarnation, or perhaps distant relatives from his own past.

6) He realizes he has a choice to make. He would have to enter the cave at either the left or at the right. Without making any conscious choice, he is soon drawn into the cave on the left. He quickly zooms past the immobile figure into dark tunnels leading deeper into the cliffs.

# 16 DELIGHT (豫 YU)

| 豫 | YU Pictogram:<br><br>Elephant 象 going back and<br>forth 于 (See Wieger,<br>Lesson 95) | Meanings:<br><br>To prepare,<br>comfort, be at<br>ease |
|---|---|---|

### THUNDER over EARTH: Aroused from Dormancy

Natural: New Growth rises from the Earth
Outer Persona: Aroused
Inner Spirit: Yielding
Element: Wood
Yang over Yin (Young Yang)

### INNER ROOT GUA: #8 WATER/EARTH, UNITY
Yin over Yin (Old Yin)
Power Score = 9 (1$^{st}$ Quartile)

### Scoring Matrix

| Gua Diagram | Line | Correctness | Activation | |
|---|---|---|---|---|
| | 6 | 1 | – | 0 |
| | 5 | 0 | | |
| | 4 | 0 | – | 0 |
| | 3 | 0 | | |
| | 2 | 1 | – | 0 |
| | 1 | 0 | | |

### Power Score: 2 (4th Quartile)

- Correctness: 2
- Activation: 0
- Carrying: 0
- Centrality: 0
- Reflection: 0

### Total Dual Score: 11 (3$^{rd}$ Quartile)

## 16 DELIGHT (豫 YU)

"The Heavenly Revelation" Narrative

△ △

### Vision 64
### Descent of the Golden Pearl– The Witness

O

Delight, roused from dormancy,
Rooted in Unity

1) A diffuse, golden light surrounds the Witness as he hovers within empty, featureless space. He has no sense of body or mass though he feels enclosed within a glowing translucent bubble.

2) He begins to move. The quality of light outside changes, first becoming darker and then gradually lighter, as deep purple gives way to blue. From the direction of the stream of fuzzy shapes he sees passing by, he realizes he is traveling downwards, still wrapped in the golden orb.

3) The sensation of downward movement slows and stops. Dark green shapes hover outside. He begins to move from the center of the glowing mass towards these shapes.

4) Fully outside the sphere, which is left behind him now, he looks out across a meticulously manicured environment. He hovers above a field of close cropped, thick green grass.

5) At the end of the field, sits a row of immaculately groomed hedges. Behind them stand several rows of identical, symmetrically shaped pine trees, each row higher than the last. Rising in height, he recedes away from the trees, until the sphere he traveled in is now a visible part of the landscape.

6) He sees a large golden, glowing orb, pulsing like a miniature, shimmering sun that has come down to earth, hovering above the center of the field. The colors are shimmering and saturated, everything rendered with supranatural sharpness and clarity. The world, like him, is transfigured.

# 17 FOLLOWING (隨 SUI)

| 隨 | SUI Pictogram:<br><br>To walk 辵 plus phonetic components (See Wieger, Lesson 46) | Meanings:<br><br>To follow, to comply with, to allow |
|---|---|---|

## LAKE over THUNDER: Joyful Action

Natural: Lake nurtures new Growth
Outer Persona: Passionate
Inner Spirit: Aroused
Element: Metal (Silver)
Yin over Yang (Young Yin)

## INNER ROOT GUA: #63 WATER/FIRE, ALREADY ACROSS
Yin over Yang (Young Yin)
Power Score = 15 (1st Quartile)

### Scoring Matrix

| Gua Diagram | Line | Correctness | Activation | |
|---|---|---|---|---|
| | 6 | 1 | O | 1 |
| | 5 | 1 | | |
| | 4 | 0 | – | 0 |
| | 3 | 0 | | |
| | 2 | 1 | ★ | 2 |
| | 1 | 1 | | |

## Power Score: 9 (1st Quartile)

- Correctness: 4
- Activation: 3
- Carrying: 0
- Centrality: 2
- Reflection: 0

## Total Dual Score: 24 (1st Quartile)

## 17 FOLLOWING (隨 SUI)

"The Nexus Formation" Narrative

△ △ △ △

### Vision 3
### The Children's Pilgrimage – The Traveller
3
Following, with joyful action,
Rooted in being Already Across

1) The Traveller is located to the left of a hiking path in a clearing in the woods. The clearing is roughly oval in shape, with grasses and small bushes in it. The path, which is lined with trees, curves around the clearing.
2) He is not alone. Next to him is the Teacher, who indicates that she is in control of the events he is seeing.
3) A seemingly endless procession of children of various ages and sizes, both boys and girls, come down the path towards him. They are dressed in a wide variety of attire, displaying many different colors and textures. They disappear as they walk past him, rounding the bend.
4) The lines of children are shepherded by young adults, who, standing by the sides of the path, guide them on their way. The path is wide enough for three children to walk alongside each other, forming loose rows of three abreast.
5) Their pace, as well as their demeanor, is relaxed and carefree, with some children sometimes walking a little slower or faster than others, not always in a straight line. As a result, though their relative positions within the progression are not always fixed, the rows would periodically re-form until the next shuffling occurred.
6) To the Traveller, the pilgrimage looks like a flowing river of vibrant humanity, whose areas of ebbs and flows correspond to the jostling and intermingling movements of the children.

# 18 POISON (REMEDY) (蠱 GU)

| | GU Pictogram: | Meanings: |
|---|---|---|
| 蠱 | Multiple worms 虫 in a vessel 皿 (See Wieger, Lesson 110) | Insanity, poison |

### MOUNTAIN over WIND: Bound to Dissolution

Natural: Winds blowing around Mountain
Outer Persona: Stubborn
Inner Spirit: Focused
Element: Earth
Yang over Yin (Young Yang)

INNER ROOT GUA: #64 FIRE/WATER,
NOT YET ACROSS
Yang over Yin (Young Yang)
Power Score = 1 (4th Quartile)

## Scoring Matrix

| Gua Diagram | Line | Correctness | Activation | |
|---|---|---|---|---|
| | 6 | 0 | – | 0 |
| | 5 | 0 | | |
| | 4 | 1 | O | 1 |
| | 3 | 1 | | |
| | 2 | 0 | – | 0 |
| | 1 | 0 | | |

## Power Score: 4 (3rd Quartile)

- Correctness: 2
- Activation: 1
- Carrying: 0
- Centrality: 1
- Reflection: 0

## Total Dual Score: 5 (4th Quartile)

# 18 POISON (REMEDY) (蠱 GU)

"The Soul Revelation" Narrative

Δ

## Vision 49
### The Demon Dismissal – The Seeker
1

Poison, bound to dissolution,
Rooted in being Not Yet Across

1) The Seeker sits in his room, meditating. Sinking deeper into trance but still aware of himself and his environment, he sees a face coming into focus, floating before him, as if he is looking into a mirror.
2) The face is that of a younger man, long and narrow with angular cheekbones, dark eyes and straight brown hair.
3) He soon realizes that he is seeing an image of his own face when he was about 35 years old. Following this recognition, the features of the face begin to morph into something else.
4) The overall shape of the face distorts into a twisted version of itself. The mouth develops a sneer. The eye sockets become hollowed out and blackened around the edges, as if the eye had been burned out from within. The hair becomes wild and protrudes in snake-like clumps.
5) A demon-like visage is now glaring back at him. In spite of its horrific appearance, he feels no emotion or apprehension, only a strange calmness.
6) But his instincts tell him some response is required. He flexes some previously undiscovered internal muscles and with the gesture of an imaginary hand, sweeps the image of the demon away. He feels some satisfaction from this.

# 19 APPROACHING (臨 LIN)

| | LIN Pictogram: | Meanings: |
|---|---|---|
| 臨 | To recline 卧 with group of people 品 (See Wieger, Lesson 82) | To face, to arrive, to overlook |

### EARTH over LAKE: Yielding to Emotion

Natural: Swamp next to Lake
Outer Persona: Yielding
Inner Spirit: Passionate
Element: Earth
Yin over Yin (Old Yin)

### INNER ROOT GUA: #51 THUNDER/THUNDER, TAKING ACTION
Yang over Yang (Old Yang)
Power Score = 4 (3$^{rd}$ Quartile)

### Scoring Matrix

| Gua Diagram | Line | Correctness | Activation | |
|---|---|---|---|---|
| | 6 | 1 | – | 0 |
| | 5 | 0 | | |
| | 4 | 1 | O | 1 |
| | 3 | 0 | | |
| | 2 | 0 | – | 0 |
| | 1 | 1 | | |

## Power Score: 5 (3rd Quartile)

- Correctness: 3
- Activation: 1
- Carrying: 0
- Centrality: 1
- Reflection: 0

## Total Dual Score: 9 (3$^{rd}$ Quartile)

# 19 APPROACHING (臨 LIN)

"The Dragon Encounter" Narrative

△ △

## Vision 11
### In Search of the Mystery – The First Son
1

Approaching, yielding to emotion,
Rooted in Taking Action

1) The First Son walks on a dirt path surrounded by a lush tropical jungle. The sunlight is dappled due to its passage through the thick canopy above and somewhat diminished by the edges of the surrounding cliffs

2) Following behind him is a group of dark skinned, shorthaired boys dressed in little more than loincloths wrapped around their waists. The older boys wear beaded neckpieces. Similarly dressed, his neckpiece is larger and more ornamental. They all look to him for leadership.

3) They move fairly briskly along the downward sloping path, on the way to the low-lying swamp at the edge of the forest to investigate the rumors of a sighting of some strange crocodile-like beast.

4) He had been forbidden to go there by his mother, the tribe's Spirit Walker and Queen, and the War Chief, his father, because it would be too dangerous. He doesn't understand the fuss.

5) After jogging at an easy pace for a while, the group nears the swamp. They feel no sense of apprehension. This swamp forms during the rainy season when the Great River overflows its banks. The path grows soft and muddy.

6) The jungle grows brighter as more light from the sun penetrates the canopy thinned by frequent flooding. Looking ahead they see the beginnings of the swamp in the distance. They peer over the still waters looking for any signs of life. Aside from some gently approaching wavelets at the far edge of the swamp, they spy nothing out of the ordinary.

# 20 OBSERVING (觀 GUAN)

| | GUAN Pictogram: | Meanings: |
|---|---|---|
| 觀 | As a stork 雚 sees 见 (See Wieger, Lesson 103) | To look at, observe, watch |

### WIND over EARTH: Focused Receptivity

Natural: Wings over the Earth
Outer Persona: Focused
Inner Spirit: Yielding
Element: Wood
Yin over Yin (Old Yin)

### INNER ROOT GUA: #52 MOUNTAIN/MOUNTAIN, KEEPING STILL
Yang over Yang (Old Yang)
Power Score = 4 (3rd Quartile)

### Scoring Matrix

| Gua Diagram | Line | Correctness | Activation | |
|---|---|---|---|---|
| | 6 | 0 | – | 0 |
| | 5 | 1 | | |
| | 4 | 1 | – | 0 |
| | 3 | 0 | | |
| | 2 | 1 | O | 1 |
| | 1 | 0 | | |

## Power Score: 7 (2nd Quartile)

- Correctness: 3
- Activation: 1
- Carrying: 1
- Centrality: 2
- Reflection: 0

## Total Dual Score: 11 (3rd Quartile)

# 20 OBSERVING (觀 GUAN)

"The Nexus Formation" Narrative

Δ Δ

## Vision 1
## The Wings of Flight – The Rider
1
Observing, focused receptivity,
Rooted in Keeping Still

1) Thick foliage and low hanging willow branches surround the Rider in his backyard. He is watching a bird in flight. The bird glides over the creek, with sharply pointed wings held at an acute angle. The leading edge of the underside of the wings is a dark, greyish blue, while the bottom edge is reddish brown.

2) Suddenly, he is no longer standing in his backyard looking up at the bird. Instead, he finds himself quickly rising up through the tree branches. He is flying. Has he become the very bird he was watching?

3) He is soon far above what should have been his neighborhood, but wasn't. Arrayed below him are brightly colored rows of small cottages made up of stucco-like cob material. The roofs are a thatched material, darker but also colored. There are dirt and gravel roads winding among the rows of cottages. He feels that this is his territory.

4) Even though he is flying and suspended beneath two large wings, he soon realizes he is not a bird. His head is perched on a long neck, his body smooth and featherless, and he has two legs and arms tucked beneath him.

5) In spite of his present state, he recognizes the objects below him as human houses and roads. He soon is flying much closer to the ground, traveling up a steep hill over a dirt road just above the roofs of the cottages lining the road to his right.

6) He climbs a hill very much like the one in his neighborhood. It ends at a forested area, with meadows and groves of redwood and oak trees and footpaths leading into its interior.

## 21 ERADICATING (噬嗑 SHI KE)

| 噬嗑 | SHI KE Pictogram:<br><br>Mouths 口 with phonetics | Meanings:<br><br>SHI: to bite, devour<br>KE: crack seeds with teeth |
|---|---|---|

### FIRE over THUNDER: Consuming Action

Natural: Fire consumes new Growth
Outer Persona: Excited
Inner Spirit: Aroused
Element: Fire
Yang over Yang (Old Yang)

### INNER ROOT GUA: #42 WIND/THUNDER, INCREASING
Yin over Yang (Young Yin)
Power Score = 10 (1st Quartile)

### Scoring Matrix

| Gua Diagram | Line | Correctness | Activation | |
|---|---|---|---|---|
| | 6 | 0 | – | 0 |
| | 5 | 0 | | |
| | 4 | 0 | – | 0 |
| | 3 | 0 | | |
| | 2 | 1 | O | 1 |
| | 1 | 1 | | |

### Power Score: 3 (4th Quartile)

- Correctness: 2
- Activation: 1
- Carrying: 0
- Centrality: 0
- Reflection: 0

### Total Dual Score: 13 (2nd Quartile)

# 21 ERADICATING (噬嗑 SHI KE)

"The Soul Revelation" Narrative

Δ Δ Δ

## Vision 47
## The Hour of the Wolf – The Seeker
1
Eradicating, with consuming action,
Rooted in Increase

1) The Seeker, in trance, sees a younger version of himself, laying flat on the ground, back pressed against a sparsely grassed field, arms by his sides, palms up. This Other-Self is alive but not moving, his eyes closed. His demeanor appears contemplative, yoga-like, as if he awaits the arrival of some kind of revelation.

2) From the Seeker's point of view, the scene is seen in perspective, with the subject's feet pointed towards the lower left and his head towards the upper right.

3) A large grey white Wolf saunters into view from the right side of the scene. She moves lazily, not showing any haste or excitement, languid in her movements.

4) After circling the body a few times, always in a counter-clockwise direction, the Wolf stops below the body, her nose facing the Other-Self's head.

5) As the Seeker watches, the Wolf begins to feed on the head of the Other-Self, apparently intent on devouring his face. The Other-Self, surprisingly, continues to remain still, showing no reaction to what's happening to him.

6) Even though the Seeker's perspective is now fluctuating between that of the observing witness and the subject of the Wolf's attention, he feels no pain or fear. When occupying the body of the Other-Self, he lies there calmly with eyes closed. He floats within a reddish dark void, feeling only a vague, distant, shaking pressure on his head.

# 22 ADORNMENT (賁 BI)

| 賁 | BI Pictogram:<br><br>Plants 卉 and shells 貝<br>(See Wieger, Lesson 78) | Meanings:<br><br>BI: bright, ornaments<br>FEN: luxurious, abundant |
|---|---|---|

MOUNTAIN over FIRE: Stopped by Brightness

Natural: Fires below the Mountain
Outer Persona: Stubborn
Inner Spirit: Excited
Element: Earth
Yang over Yang (Old Yang)

INNER ROOT GUA: #41 MOUNTAIN/LAKE,
DECREASING
Yang over Yin (Young Yang)
Power Score = 4 (3rd Quartile)

## Scoring Matrix

| Gua Diagram | Line | Correctness | Activation | |
|---|---|---|---|---|
| | 6 | 0 | – | 0 |
| | 5 | 0 | | |
| | 4 | 1 | ★ | 2 |
| | 3 | 1 | | |
| | 2 | 1 | O | 1 |
| | 1 | 1 | | |

## Power Score: 7 (2nd Quartile)

- Correctness: 4
- Activation: 3
- Carrying: 0
- Centrality: 0
- Reflection: 0

## Total Dual Score: 11 (3rd Quartile)

## 22 ADORNMENT (賁 BI)

"The Soul Revelation" Narrative

Δ Δ

### Vision 53
### A Touch of Flowers – The Seeker
3
Adornment, stopped by brightness,
Rooted in Decrease

1) The Seeker is sitting in his room, meditating. Sinking deeper into trance, he sees the crown of someone's head beginning to take shape.

2) From his perspective, it is as if he has rotated 90 degrees to his left and is hovering above the head, while looking directly down at its top.

3) The hair is short and tightly curled. Its color initially is jet black. As he watches, its surface begins to shimmer.

4) Where before there was a solid black mass of hair, there is now a field of 6-sided, star-shaped flowers starting to propagate across its curved surface. Each flower is a different color from the ones adjacent to it. All are the same size and shape.

5) Soon the entire head is covered by a jigsaw-like pattern of multi-colored star blossoms. The pointed pedals of each flower are in complete contact with those of all adjacent ones, with no empty space visible between them.

6) Curious as to its texture, the Seeker reaches down with a hand to touch its surface. It still feels like hair to him, having a bristly, spongy like texture to it, reminding the Seeker of how his beard feels. He realizes that he is looking at the head of a magical being, the Vision Dancer of the Fire Ritual.

## 23 SPLITTING APART (剝 BO)

| 剝 | BO Pictogram:<br><br>Carve tree 彔 with knife 刀<br>(See Wieger, Lesson 68) | Meanings:<br><br>To peel, to skin |
|---|---|---|

### MOUNTAIN over EARTH: Resistant Yielding

Natural: Mountains on the Plains
Outer Persona: Stubborn
Inner Spirit: Yielding
Element: Earth
Yang over Yin (Young Yang)

### INNER ROOT GUA: #23 MOUNTAIN/EARTH, SPLITTING APART
Yang over Yin (Young Yang)
Power Score = 2 (4th Quartile)

### Scoring Matrix

| Gua Diagram | Line | Correctness | Activation | |
|---|---|---|---|---|
| | 6 | 0 | – | 0 |
| | 5 | 0 | | |
| | 4 | 1 | – | 0 |
| | 3 | 0 | | |
| | 2 | 1 | – | 0 |
| | 1 | 0 | | |

### Power Score: 2 (4th Quartile)

- Correctness: 2
- Activation: 0
- Carrying: 0
- Centrality: 0
- Reflection: 0

### Total Dual Score: 4 (4th Quartile)

# 23 SPLITTING APART (剝 BO)

"The Soul Revelation" Narrative

Δ

## Vision 54
## The Stranger Self– The Seeker

O

Splitting Apart, with resistant yielding,
Rooted in more Splitting Apart

1) The Seeker is sitting in his room in the transitional phase of meditation. Slipping deeper into trance, but still aware of himself and his situation, he sees a face beginning to form. It hovers before him like a face the Seeker would see in a mirror.

2) The individual has grey and white streaked hair, a narrow face, and a predominantly white beard.

3) His demeanor suggests that he is actively looking at the Seeker, trying to determine if he recognizes him. His manner suggests that he does not.

4) This is not the case for the Seeker. He is also actively examining the face before him, but he is doing so precisely because it does look so familiar to him.

5) It finally dawns on the Seeker that what is before him is actually an accurate image of his current self, the very one he sees in a mirror every day, and not the much younger one remembered from his other visions.

6) The Other-Self before him has a different reaction regarding what he is seeing. He looks directly at the Seeker and says, "Who are you? Identify yourself."

## 24 TURNING BACK (復 FU)

| 復 | FU Pictogram:<br><br>Step 彳 and repeat 复<br>(See Wieger, Lesson 75) | Meanings:<br><br>Repeat, return |
|---|---|---|

### EARTH over THUNDER: Yielding Action

Natural: New Growth begins Underground
Outer Persona: Yielding
Inner Spirit: Aroused
Element: Earth
Yin over Yang (Young Yin)

### INNER ROOT GUA: #24 EARTH/THUNDER, TURNING BACK
Yin over Yang (Young Yin)
Power Score = 6 (2nd Quartile)

### Scoring Matrix

| Gua Diagram | Line | Correctness | Activation | |
|---|---|---|---|---|
| | 6 | 1 | – | 0 |
| | 5 | 0 | | |
| | 4 | 1 | O | 1 |
| | 3 | 0 | | |
| | 2 | 1 | O | 1 |
| | 1 | 1 | | |

### Power Score: 6 (2nd Quartile)

- Correctness: 4
- Activation: 2
- Carrying: 0
- Centrality: 0
- Reflection: 0

### Total Dual Score: 12 (3rd Quartile)

## 24 TURNING BACK (復 FU)

"The Pyramid Ascension" Narrative

Δ Δ

### Vision 37
### The Council of Elders – The Traveller
2

Turning Back, with yielding action,
Rooted in more Turning Back

1) The Traveller enters a glass chamber suspended on beams within a circular white tower. Turning around, he discovers the Teacher. She directs his attention to the walls of the chamber. He now stands in a square white room containing only a single Blue Door.

2) The Teacher opens the door and leads him down a long white corridor with doors on both sides. She stops and opens a door on the left, indicating that he should go inside.

3) The room contains a large rectangular table stretching back to the far wall. The walls are covered floor to ceiling with overflowing bookshelves. Seated around the table are nine white bearded, distinguished looking gentlemen, four on each side and one at the far end, the Magister.

4) He notices an empty chair at the end of the table near him. Standing up, the Magister welcomes him to the Council of Elders and gestures for him to sit.

5) The Traveller looks down and recognizes a much younger version of himself. He feels too young and inexperienced to be in their presence. Turning to leave, he says, "I don't belong here. I'm only a Neophyte."

6) Walking away, the Teacher by his side, he hears the Magister say, "You are much more than that, Traveller. No matter where you go or who you are, your journey will always bring you back here."

# 25 TRUTH (無妄 WU WANG)

| 無妄 | WU WANG Pictogram: Without 無 fleeing 亡 woman 女 | Meanings: WU: without WANG: absurd, fantastic |
|---|---|---|

### HEAVEN over THUNDER: Power of Arousal

Natural: New Growth reaches for the Sky
Outer Persona: Engaged
Inner Spirit: Aroused
Element: Metal (Gold)
Yang over Yang (Old Yang)

INNER ROOT GUA: #37 WIND/FIRE,
THE FAMILY
Yin over Yang (Young Yin)
Power Score = 12 (1$^{st}$ Quartile)

### Scoring Matrix

| Gua Diagram | Line | Correctness | Activation | |
|---|---|---|---|---|
| | 6 | 0 | – | 0 |
| | 5 | 1 | | |
| | 4 | 0 | – | 0 |
| | 3 | 0 | | |
| | 2 | 1 | ★ | 2 |
| | 1 | 1 | | |

## Power Score: 7 (2nd Quartile)

- Correctness: 3
- Activation: 2
- Carrying: 0
- Centrality: 2
- Reflection: 0

## Total Dual Score: 19 (1st Quartile)

# 25 TRUTH (無妄 WU WANG)

"The Pyramid Ascension" Narrative

△ △ △ △

## Vision 31
### The Prism of Rainbow Light – The Seeker
2

Truth, through power of arousal,
Rooted in Family

1) Sitting in meditative trance, the Seeker sees a blank white region spread out before him. In its center a translucent, triangular shaped object begins to form, with three sides of equal length.

2) As he is pulled closer and closer to this object, he recognizes that it is a glass prism, with two flat extruded sides and a base.

3) Now he is inside the object. Looking diagonally up and out the left and right sides, he sees nothing outside the prism but empty white space.

4) Within the prism a diffuse sphere of golden light begins to form around him. As the sphere of light grows brighter, it starts to coalesce, become more opaque. Rays flow out from it, illuminating more of the prism's interior.

5) Once the inside of the prism is totally engulfed in this golden light, the prism itself begins to transform. Its sides grow and fold around each other, until what remains is a four-sided translucent pyramid enclosing the pulsing golden light.

6) This light now spreads out through the pyramid's four walls. The Seeker sees that for each side, spectrums of multicolored spheres of light are projected upwards and outwards, bathing the once empty space in shimmering rays of incandescent colors.

## 26 GREAT ACCUMULATION (大畜 DA CHU)

| 大畜 | DA CHU Pictogram: Large 大 covered 玄 fields 田 (farm) (See Wieger, Lesson 91) | Meanings: Large fields of livestock |
|---|---|---|

### MOUNTAIN over HEAVEN: Aggregating Power

Natural: Mountain towering above the Sky
Outer Persona: Stubborn
Inner Spirit: Engaged
Element: Earth
Yang over Yang (Old Yang)

INNER ROOT GUA: #38 FIRE/LAKE, ALIENATION
Yang over Yin (Young Yang)
Power Score = 2 (4$^{th}$ Quartile)

### Scoring Matrix

| Gua Diagram | Line | Correctness | Activation | |
|---|---|---|---|---|
| | 6 | 0 | – | 0 |
| | 5 | 0 | | |
| | 4 | 1 | ★ | 2 |
| | 3 | 1 | | |
| | 2 | 0 | – | 0 |
| | 1 | 1 | | |

### Power Score: 6 (2nd Quartile)

- Correctness: 3
- Activation: 2
- Carrying: 0
- Centrality: 1
- Reflection: 0

### Total Dual Score: 8 (4th Quartile)

# 26 GREAT ACCUMULATION (大畜 DA CHU)

"The Nexus Formation" Narrative

Δ

## Vision 2
### The Spirit Condensation – The Traveller
2
Great Accumulation, with aggregating power,
Rooted in Alienation

1) The Traveller walks on a dirt path surrounded by oaks and pines and some scattered redwood trees. Heavy underbrush lines the sides of the path. The sky is a bright blue. No other persons or animals are visible

2) As he comes around a corner curving to the left, he sees a sharply sloping drop-off to his right overlooking grassy meadows visible a few hillsides below. Sunlight streams through the trees dappling the path.

3) As he looks to the open area on his right, he sees a shower of whitish fuzzy particles beginning to drift down from the otherwise clear blue sky. Wave after wave of these translucent flakes slowly drift down from above. There are neither clouds visible nor any perceptible currents of wind.

4) Even though the air is warm and still, he feels like he is in the midst of a flurry of ephemeral snowflakes. It is as if a field of dandelions strewn across some heavenly alpine meadow has decided to give up its seeds in one prolific burst.

5) None of these particles accumulate on the ground, nor did any seem to fall on him, in spite of the fact that they are tumbling and drifting all around him.

6) He thinks to himself that this must be what it is like to dodge raindrops, albeit slow and lazy ones. Whatever these objects are, they seem to disappear when they get close to him or to the ground.

# 27 NOURISHING (頤 YI)

| | YI Pictogram: | Meanings: |
|---|---|---|
| 頤 | Cheeks with head (See Wieger, Lesson 29) | Cheeks, nourish |

### MOUNTAIN over THUNDER: Stilling Arousal

Natural: New Growth at base of Mountain
Outer Persona: Stubborn
Inner Spirit: Aroused
Element: Earth
Yang over Yang (Old Yang)

### INNER ROOT GUA: #27 MOUNTAIN/THUNDER, NOURISHING
Yang over Yang (Old Yang)
Power Score = 6 (2nd Quartile)

### Scoring Matrix

| Gua Diagram | Line | Correctness | Activation | |
|---|---|---|---|---|
| | 6 | 0 | – | 0 |
| | 5 | 0 | | |
| | 4 | 1 | O | 1 |
| | 3 | 0 | | |
| | 2 | 1 | O | 1 |
| | 1 | 1 | | |

### Power Score: 6 (2nd Quartile)
- Correctness: 3
- Activation: 2
- Carrying: 0
- Centrality: 0
- Reflection: 1

### Total Dual Score: 12 (3rd Quartile)

# 27 NOURISHING (頤 YI)

## "The Heavenly Revelation" Narrative

Δ Δ

### Vision 56
### Breath of the Inner Sun – The Seeker
2
Nourishing, stilling of arousal,
Rooted in more Nourishing

1) Out in the mundane world, the Seeker sits in a Waiting Room, along with several others, who, like him, are patiently waiting to be called into another room for their appointments.

2) Surrounded by plastic chairs and overhead fluorescent lights, the Seeker realizes this is not the ideal place for meditation. Nonetheless, he closes his eyes, orients his body into a relaxed pose, and begins to breath slowly.

3) Following his Practice, he focuses on the shifting amorphous shapes in the dark fields arrayed behind his closed eyelids.

4) In the center of this field, an orange-yellow orb of light begins to form. As he watches, this orb grows in size and morphs into a larger, more diffuse, duller orange-red orb. These two are not really distinct states, but are instead the end points of a continuous and cyclic process of change.

5) This transitioning between bright yellow and dull red states soon becomes a repeating rhythmic cycle, one on which he is able to focus his complete attention without causing any disruption.

6) He soon realizes that the cycles are coordinated with his breathing, bright orange-yellow on the inhalation, and dull orange-red on the exhalation. This pattern seems significant to him. The phenomenon continues without interruption until he opens his eyes.

# 28 GREAT CROSSING (大過 DA GUO)

| 大過 | DA GUO Pictogram: Great 大 moving 辵 (See Wieger, Lesson 91) | Meanings: Great going, crossing over |
|---|---|---|

## LAKE over WIND: Joyful Entry

Natural: Trees growing in Lake
Outer Persona: Passionate
Inner Spirit: Focused
Element: Metal (Silver)
Yin over Yin (Old Yin)

INNER ROOT GUA: #28 LAKE/WIND
GREAT CROSSING
Yin over Yin (Old Yin)
Power Score = 8 (2nd Quartile)

### Scoring Matrix

| Gua Diagram | Line | Correctness | Activation | |
|---|---|---|---|---|
| | 6 | 1 | ★ | 2 |
| | 5 | 1 | | |
| | 4 | 0 | – | 0 |
| | 3 | 1 | | |
| | 2 | 0 | – | 0 |
| | 1 | 0 | | |

## Power Score: 8 (2nd Quartile)

- Correctness: 3
- Activation: 2
- Carrying: 0
- Centrality: 2
- Reflection: 1

## Total Dual Score: 16 (1st Quartile)

# 28 GREAT CROSSING (大過 DA GUO)

"The Heavenly Revelation" Narrative

△ △ △ △

## Vision 62
### Visiting the Master – The Traveller
2

Great Crossing, with joyful entry,
Rooted in further Great Crossing

1) The Traveller walks down a long corridor in a building where everything is painted white. The corridor winds its way through the stark structure, which is laid out more like a labyrinth than the floor plan of a normal building. At first he sees no doors. Finally, the Traveller comes to a section of the corridor in which brown doors begin to sporadically dot the sides of the hallway.

2) Turning a corner, he sees on his left a door that is different from the others. It is blue in color rather than generic brown. It also has a silver colored doorknob instead of bronze.

3) He opens the door to enter a large, richly furnished room, which reminds him of a scholar's study or library. Tall shelves line the walls and an ornate rug sits before a crackling fireplace. Two over-stuffed chairs face the fireplace, which is located on the far wall across from the door.

4) Entering further into the room he sees that one of the chairs is occupied. A well-appointed older gentleman sits there, with grey hair and a white beard, wearing a tweed, three-piece grey suit. He indicates that the Traveller should sit in the empty chair.

5) As the Traveller settles in, the man looks at him and says, "So you're back. You've found me once again." The Traveller nods, though not sure what the man means. He then realizes the man is the Magister he has met before.

6) The Magister pauses and adds, "Very good. I can see that you remember. Shall we begin? I have Six Impossible Things to tell you and your time here is short."

# 29 THE PIT (DARKNESS) (坎 KAN)

| 坎 | KAN Pictogram:<br><br>Ground 土 inducing<br><br>exhalation 欠<br>(See Wieger, Lesson 99) | Meanings:<br><br>Pit, threshold |
|---|---|---|

### WATER over WATER: Swimming in Darkness

Natural: Deep, fast Rivers
Outer Persona: Immersed
Inner Spirit: Immersed
Element: Water
Yin over Yin (Old Yin)

### INNER ROOT GUA: #62 THUNDER/MOUNTAIN, SMALL CROSSING
Yang over Yang (Old Yang)
Power Score = 5 (3$^{rd}$ Quartile)

### Scoring Matrix

| Gua Diagram | Line | Correctness | Activation | |
|---|---|---|---|---|
| | 6 | 1 | O | 1 |
| | 5 | 1 | | |
| | 4 | 1 | – | 0 |
| | 3 | 0 | | |
| | 2 | 0 | – | 0 |
| | 1 | 0 | | |

## Power Score: 8 (2$^{nd}$ Quartile)

- Correctness: 3
- Activation: 1
- Carrying: 1
- Centrality: 2
- Reflection: 1

## Total Dual Score: 13 (2nd Quartile)

# 29 THE PIT (DARKNESS) (坎 KAN)

### "The Spirit Incursion" Narrative

△ △ △

## Vision 44
### Lost in the Dark Abyss – The Seeker
1
The Pit, swimming in darkness,
Rooted in Small Crossing

1) The Seeker is sitting in meditation lost in deep trance, unaware of himself or his surroundings. As if a switch has been flicked, his consciousness suddenly blossoms into being, but only as a primitive awareness of raw presence.

2) This presence brings no sense of self or identity, no thoughts or feelings, no physical sensations. These aspects manifest themselves entirely as a sense of absence, leaving only the barest form of a being-here-now.

3) The "here" is as much of a mystery to his awareness as the mystery of his identity is. The pervading mystery is all there is, a mystery which manifests itself in sensation in the form of a deep, black, empty void – a blackness deeper than black.

4) After an indeterminate amount of time passes in this dark emptiness, a small flame springs into life. It takes the form of a single thought: "Where am I?"

5) Whatever the source of this thought, it serves as the seed for the genesis of a more expansive awareness. He remembers where he is and soon thereafter who he is.

6) His sense of physical form likewise begins to return, but strangely not as a body sitting in his meditation chair. Rather, he feels as if his body is hovering in space to the left of the chair.

# 30 FIRE (離 LI)

| 離 | LI Pictogram:<br><br>Bird 隹 with phonetic<br>(See Wieger, Lesson 168) | Meanings:<br><br>To leave,<br>depart, go away |
|---|---|---|

## FIRE over FIRE: Clinging Brightness

Natural: Massive Fire
Outer Persona: Excited
Inner Spirit: Excited
Element: Fire
Yang over Yang (Old Yang)

INNER ROOT GUA: #61 WIND/LAKE,
INNER TRUTH
Yin over Yin (Old Yin)
Power Score = 8 (2$^{nd}$ Quartile)

## Scoring Matrix

| Gua Diagram | Line | Correctness | Activation | |
|---|---|---|---|---|
| | 6 | 0 | – | 0 |
| | 5 | 0 | | |
| | 4 | 0 | – | 0 |
| | 3 | 1 | | |
| | 2 | 1 | O | 1 |
| | 1 | 1 | | |

## Power Score: 5 (3rd Quartile)

- Correctness: 3
- Activation: 1
- Carrying: 0
- Centrality: 0
- Reflection: 1

## Total Dual Score: 13 (2nd Quartile)

# 30 FIRE (離 LI)

## "The Spirit Incursion" Narrative
## △ △ △
### Vision 40
### Flight of the Firebird – The Seeker
1
Fire, clinging to brightness,
Rooted in Inner Truth

1) The Seeker has ended the meditation session in which the Descent had occurred.

2) Back in the mundane world, he has left his meditation room and gone downstairs, where he is standing next to the side window by the dining room table. He is still somewhat shaken by the events of his session.

3) He looks over the deck past the nearby trees towards the adjacent pond, as he tries to understand the nature of what he had just experienced. Suddenly something catches his eye as a bird zips by the window over the deck.

4) Now on alert, he notices more detail about the bird as it quickly returns, flying in a tight loop near the window.

5) The bird is medium sized and a brilliant, solid scarlet red in color. Its wings are sharply angled and its head pointed, making it look almost like a miniature fighter jet.

6) The bird continues to fly tight aerobatic turns and spins and loops in front of the window for about thirty seconds before disappearing, never to be seen again. He has the distinct impression that this performance was specifically intended for him.

# 31 INFLUENCE (咸 XIAN)

| 咸 | XIAN Pictogram:<br>Wound 戌 with mouth 口<br>(See Wieger, Lesson 71)<br>(or GAN, possibly missing radical for heart) | Meanings:<br>XIAN: All, in all cases, together; GAN: Affect, move, touch |
|---|---|---|

LAKE over MOUNTAIN: Joyful Tranquility

Natural: High Mountain Lake
Outer Persona: Passionate
Inner Spirit: Stubborn
Element: Metal (Silver)
Yin over Yang (Young Yin)

INNER ROOT GUA: #48 WATER/WIND,
REPLENISHING
Yin over Yin (Old Yin)
Power Score = 10 (1st Quartile)

## Scoring Matrix

| Gua Diagram | Line | Correctness | Activation | |
|---|---|---|---|---|
| | 6 | 1 | ★ | 2 |
| | 5 | 1 | | |
| | 4 | 0 | – | 0 |
| | 3 | 1 | | |
| | 2 | 1 | O | 1 |
| | 1 | 0 | | |

## Power Score: 9 (1st Quartile)

- Correctness: 4
- Activation: 3
- Carrying: 0
- Centrality: 2
- Reflection: 0

## Total Dual Score: 19 (1st Quartile)

# 31 INFLUENCE (咸 XIAN)

"The Spirit Incursion" Narrative

△ △ △ △

Vision 38

## Lights in the Darkness – The Seeker

3

Influence, with joyful tranquility,
Rooted in Replenishing

1) The Seeker sits in his room, meditating. He is still present in the mundane world, feeling his body and aware of his surroundings. Following his practice, he stares at the shifting dark shapes drifting behind his closed eyes.
2) As his breathing slows, he slips deeper into the first stages of the meditational trance.
3) Suddenly there is a bright flash of orange-yellow light. It briefly illuminates his entire visual field before quickly fading out. It disappears as quickly as it had appeared.
4) As if the first pulse was a test firing, the flash returns again, and this time persists, blinking quickly on and off with a constant frequency, each pulse lasting about a second. This continues for about thirty seconds.
5) The flashing occurs at a pace driven by its own internal rhythm. It is not coordinated with either his heart rate or breathing cycles, as might have been expected.
6) What drives this phenomenon remains a mystery, even as it continues to sporadically appear as an element in subsequent meditation sessions.

## 32 PERSEVERANCE (恆 HENG)

| 恆 | HENG Pictogram:<br><br>Heart 心 that extends all<br><br>the way across 亙<br>(See Wieger, Lesson 2) | Meanings:<br><br>Permanent,<br>enduring, persevere |
|---|---|---|

### THUNDER over WIND: Active Passage

Natural: New Growth rising in the Forest
Outer Persona: Aroused
Inner Spirit: Focused
Element: Wood
Yang over Yin (Young Yang)

### INNER ROOT GUA: #47 LAKE/WATER, EXHAUSTING
Yin over Yin (Old Yin)
Power Score = 5 (3rd Quartile)

### Scoring Matrix

| Gua Diagram | Line | Correctness | Activation | |
|---|---|---|---|---|
| | 6 | 1 | O | 1 |
| | 5 | 0 | | |
| | 4 | 0 | – | 0 |
| | 3 | 1 | | |
| | 2 | 0 | – | 0 |
| | 1 | 0 | | |

### Power Score: 4 (3rd Quartile)

- Correctness: 2
- Activation: 1
- Carrying: 0
- Centrality: 1
- Reflection: 0

### Total Dual Score: 9 (3rd Quartile)

# 32 PERSEVERANCE (恆 HENG)

"The Pyramid Ascension" Narrative

Δ Δ

## Vision 33
### Advancement to Candidacy – The Adept
1

Perseverance, with active passage,
Rooted in Exhausting

1) The Adept, dressed in short-sleeved white tunic and baggy pants, stands on a dirt-covered field, staring at the pyramid in the distance.

2) Surrounding him on all sides are dozens of his peers, all identically dressed. All have dark brown skin and short black hair and are androgynous in appearance.

3) But these individuals do not just look alike. He notices that their appearance is identical in all respects, as would be the case if they were identical twins or clones.

4) In the distance he sees several much taller individuals dressed similarly to him and carrying short staffs. They're involved in some kind of selection process, in which they walk up to certain Adepts and tap them on the shoulder with the staff. When they do this, the Adept would immediately collapse to the ground.

5) He asks one of the nearby Adepts what is happening. Are these fallen Adepts dead or hurt? The other Adept replies that today is "Selection Day." He is not sure if that is a good thing or a bad thing. Is he worthy of advancement?

6) Soon, he sees one of the Selectors heading directly for him. As the Selector comes up to him, the Selector nods, and then taps him on the shoulder. He feels himself crumbling to the ground, but even as his consciousness slips away, he feels no fear.

# 33 RETREAT (遁 DUN)

| 遁 | DUN Pictogram:<br><br>To walk 辶 with shield 盾<br>(See Wieger, Lesson 158) | Meanings:<br><br>Disappear, to escape, to flee |
|---|---|---|

HEAVEN over MOUNTAIN: Advance Blocked

Natural: Broad skies dwarfing Mountain
Outer Persona: Engaged
Inner Spirit: Stubborn
Element: Metal (Gold)
Yang over Yang (Old Yang)

INNER ROOT GUA: #57 WIND/WIND,
PROCEEDING HUMBLY
Yin over Yin (Old Yin)
Power Score = 7 (2nd Quartile)

## Scoring Matrix

| Gua Diagram | Line | Correctness | Activation | |
|---|---|---|---|---|
| | 6 | 0 | – | 0 |
| | 5 | 1 | | |
| | 4 | 0 | – | 0 |
| | 3 | 1 | | |
| | 2 | 1 | O | 1 |
| | 1 | 0 | | |

## Power Score: 6 (2nd Quartile)

- Correctness: 3
- Activation: 1
- Carrying: 0
- Centrality: 2
- Reflection: 0

## Total Dual Score: 13 (2nd Quartile)

# 33 RETREAT (遁 DUN)

"The Castle Redemption" Narrative

△ △ △

## Vision 25
### Retreat to the Castle — The Apprentice Smith

1

Retreat, with advance blocked,
Rooted in Proceeding Humbly

1) The Apprentice Blacksmith runs across the flat, rocky plateau perched high above the mountain ranges that surround it. No trees are visible, only low scrub growth and sparse.

2) Behind him are other members of the Watch, having sounded the alarm and passed through the village to rouse the recalcitrant from their beds, since the day is still young.

3) Looking to his right, he sees what looks like the entire population of the village running alongside him, both young and old, dressed in the peasant garb of everyday life.

4) The villagers looked relaxed, smiling as they run, not at all alarmed, thinking perhaps that this is just another random, unscheduled drill. Some turn to look at him, laughing at the serious expression they see portrayed on his face.

5) They are treating this event as a footrace, trying to be the first to reach the blocky, grey stonewalls of the castle sitting on the hill above them. The castle's gates are open, something that is unusual for this time of day.

6) In the sky above, the mournful cry of an ancient beast sounds, announcing the immanent arrival of the Sky Dragon. Its shadow drifts across the plateau like some black specter, creating alarm and confusion in the ranks of the now fleeing masses. The Apprentice pushes himself to run even faster, focused only on his destination, no longer glancing about.

# 34 GREAT STRENGTH (大壯 DA ZHUANG)

| 大壯 | DA ZHUANG Pictogram:<br>Great 大 scholar /<br>warrior 士 with phonetic<br>(See Wieger, Lesson 127) | Meanings:<br>To strengthen, strong, robust |
|---|---|---|

THUNDER over HEAVEN: Arousing Power

Natural: Thunder high in the Sky
Outer Persona: Aroused
Inner Spirit: Engaged
Element: Wood
Yang over Yang (Old Yang)

INNER ROOT GUA: #58 LAKE/LAKE,
JOYFUL
Yin over Yin (old Yin)
Power Score = 6 (2nd Quartile)

## Scoring Matrix

| Gua Diagram | Line | Correctness | Activation | |
|---|---|---|---|---|
| | 6 | 1 | O | 1 |
| | 5 | 0 | | |
| | 4 | 0 | – | 0 |
| | 3 | 1 | | |
| | 2 | 0 | – | 0 |
| | 1 | 1 | | |

## Power Score: 5 (3rd Quartile)

- Correctness: 3
- Activation: 1
- Carrying: 0
- Centrality: 1
- Reflection: 0

## Total Dual Score: 11 (3rd Quartile)

# 34 GREAT STRENGTH (大壯 DA ZHUANG)

"The Pyramid Ascension" Narrative

Δ Δ

## Vision 34
### Gathering of the Dragon Clan – The Adept
1

Great Strength, with arousing power,
Rooted in Joyfulness

1) The Adept, waking from his trance, finds himself walking on a broad boulevard lined with towering palm trees. The boulevard is a scene of bustling activity, with many merchants selling their wares on the side of the road.

2) He sees a great pyramid rising up like a mountain at the end of the roadway. It size is so massive that its pinnacle is lost in the low hanging clouds of a brewing storm.

3) He is accompanied by a small group of his fellow Adepts, all identical in dress and appearance to him, with brown skin and short black hair, dressed all in white. They are all bunched tightly together, seemingly unsure of themselves.

4) He is feeling strange and disoriented; his whole body is vibrating, especially his head, which felt like it contained a hive of bees. He feels like he is changing. Recovering more of his senses, he remembers that he has survived the selection process. But he has no idea what comes next.

5) Ahead of them waits a gathering of tall, heavily muscled individuals. They are not wearing the customary white tunics of their order, but are instead dressed in warrior garb, with shining gold armor. They all carry large spears and wear from what his vantage point looks like ornate green headpieces on their heads.

6) As he gets closer he realizes that these are not helmets, for he can now see now their true face. They stand upright, but they are not entirely human. Their heads are the heads of dragons. From his training, he knows them as the Dragon Clan.

# 35 PROGRESS (晉 JIN)

| 晉 | JIN Pictogram:<br><br>Sun 日 and swooping birds 至<br>(See Wieger, Lesson 133) | Meanings:<br><br>To advance, increase, flourish |
|---|---|---|

## FIRE over EARTH: Illumination Received

Natural: Sun warming the Earth
Outer Persona: Excited
Inner Spirit: Yielding
Element: Fire
Yang over Yin (Young Yang)

INNER ROOT GUA: #20 WIND/EARTH,
OBSERVING
Yin over Yin (Old Yin)
Power Score = 7 (2nd Quartile)

### Scoring Matrix

| Gua Diagram | Line | Correctness | Activation | |
|---|---|---|---|---|
| | 6 | 0 | – | 0 |
| | 5 | 0 | | |
| | 4 | 0 | – | 0 |
| | 3 | 0 | | |
| | 2 | 1 | – | 0 |
| | 1 | 0 | | |

## Power Score: 1 (4th Quartile)

- Correctness: 1
- Activation: 0
- Carrying: 0
- Centrality: 0
- Reflection: 0

## Total Dual Score: 8 (4th Quartile)

# 35 PROGRESS (晉 JIN)

"The Heavenly Revelation" Narrative

Δ

## Vision 61
### Unlocking Heaven's Gate – The Traveller
O

Progress, with illumination received,
Rooted in Observing

1) The Traveller stands upon a broad expanse at the top of an enormous stone block structure that is so large that its lower levels are lost in the clouds. Nor can he, from where he stands, see the top of the structure that looms above him.

2) Alone on the platform, looking down he sees other climbers struggling in vain to make it up the steep steps to where he is standing.

3) The structure is circled with high walls, dark maroon in color with ornate jade symbols fashioned into its sides. The walls are composed of smooth, ceramic material. Gold trim runs across the wall's top and divides the wall into series of large panels.

4) Walking towards his right in search of an entrance, he comes across two enormous doors. Attached to the wall with golden hinges on their outside edges, the doors are covered with elaborate spiral designs woven of cast iron bars.

5) The doors tower above him. About halfway up he sees a locking mechanism with a slot for a large key. He retrieves the ornate, golden skeleton key that he had strapped to his back.

6) Successfully climbing up the external metal works to reach the panel, he inserts the key and turns it to the right. There is no reaction from the doors, but the key in his hand suddenly disappears. After a short interval his body begins to feel strange. Looking down he sees that his body is growing more and more translucent, dissolving into a mist of golden light.

# 36 CONCEALED BRILLIANCE (夷 MING YI)

| 明夷 | MING YI Pictogram:<br>Bright (sun and moon) 明<br>barbarian (man with<br>bow) 夷<br>(See Wieger, Lesson 60) | Meanings:<br><br>Light<br>darkened |
|---|---|---|

### EARTH over FIRE: Buried Illumination

Natural: Burning lava flows underground
Outer Persona: Yielding
Inner Spirit: Excited
Element: Earth
Yin over Yang (Young Yin)

INNER ROOT GUA: #19 EARTH/LAKE,
APPROACHING
Yin over Yin (Old Yin)
Power Score = 5 (3$^{rd}$ Quartile)

### Scoring Matrix

| Gua Diagram | Line | Correctness | Activation | |
|---|---|---|---|---|
| | 6 | 1 | O | 1 |
| | 5 | 0 | | |
| | 4 | 1 | ★ | 2 |
| | 3 | 1 | | |
| | 2 | 1 | O | 1 |
| | 1 | 1 | | |

## Power Score: 9 (1st Quartile)

- Correctness: 5
- Activation: 4
- Carrying: 0
- Centrality: 0
- Reflection: 0

## Total Dual Score: 14 (2nd Quartile)

# 36 CONCEALED BRILLIANCE (夷 MING YI)

"The Dragon Encounter" Narrative

△ △ △

Vision 10
## The Golden Light Descends – The Witness
4
Concealed Brilliance, with buried illumination,
Rooted in Approaching

1) The Witness is buried beneath the earth, with nothing visible on any side except for roots, dirt, and stones. He is moving in a downward direction, with his orientation fixed straight ahead.
2) Around him everything is totally black except for an illuminated area in the center of his vision. The lit area is circular in shape with edges fading off slowly into darkness, curving around him as it follows him down.
3) He does not feel that he is moving through a hole or tunnel in the ground. Instead, the ground seems liquid-like as he sinks through it, his substance having lost all corporeality.
4) Moving deeper, he is no longer surrounded by earth or stones. Instead, he is immersed within a thick tangle of vertical tree roots of varying thicknesses, ranging from several inches in width to some only as wide as a piece of string. Many of the larger roots wind continuously around each other in helical shapes similar to that of DNA.
5) When the light passes over the dull brown roots, they are illuminated in a rich golden glow. The clumps of earth and various sized stones and debris amidst the roots are similarly transformed. Occasionally, metallic rocks reflect this light back.
6) His awareness is enshrined in this golden orb of light. No other color is visible except for the pale brown hues on the periphery of the light and the golden hues ablaze in its center.

# 37 THE FAMILY (家人 JIA REN)

| 家人 | JIA REN Pictogram:<br>People 人 with roof 宀<br>over pig 豕<br>(See Wieger, Lesson 69) | Meanings:<br>Household,<br>Family,<br>home |
|---|---|---|

### WIND over FIRE: Spreading Brightness

Natural: Winds forming over a Fire
Outer Persona: Focused
Inner Spirit: Excited
Element: Wood
Yin over Yang (Young Yin)

INNER ROOT GUA: #26 MOUNTAIN/HEAVEN,
GREAT ACCUMULATION
Yang over Yang (Old Yang)
Power Score = 6 (2nd Quartile)

### Scoring Matrix

| Gua Diagram | Line | Correctness | Activation | |
|---|---|---|---|---|
| | 6 | 0 | – | 0 |
| | 5 | 1 | | |
| | 4 | 1 | ★ | 2 |
| | 3 | 1 | | |
| | 2 | 1 | ★ | 2 |
| | 1 | 1 | | |

### Power Score: 12 (1st Quartile)

- Correctness: 5
- Activation: 4
- Carrying: 1
- Centrality: 2
- Reflection: 0

### Total Dual Score: 18 (1st Quartile)

# 37 THE FAMILY (家人 JIA REN)

"The Hidden Source" Narrative

△ △ △

## Vision 17

## The Fire Ritual – The Traveller

4

The Family, by spreading brightness,
Rooted in Great Accumulation

1) The Teacher stands before the Traveller in a dimly lit rock tunnel. She leads him through it into a large cave. Water trickles down its sides, forming a viscous black pool towards the back.

2) In the center of the cave a large bonfire is burning. Concentric circles of primitively dressed women sit around it. They are loudly drumming and chanting in a language he does not recognize. Suddenly everything stops.

3) As if on cue, everyone shouts and jumps to their feet, waving their hands over their heads with arms outstretched. A figure materializes next to the fire's surging flames, the Vision Dancer. She has dark features and black hair and for clothing wears only strips of leather across her top and bottom.

4) As the crowd chants and stomps and drums, the mysterious figure starts to spin in wild gyrations, flinging her body around the fire in ecstatic frenzy. The faster she moves and spins, the higher the flames surge.

5) Some movement inside the white smoke rising from the fire grabs his attention. He sees a 3-D image forming inside it, which as he watches soon resolves into a vivid, real time, and holographic-like image of the scene occurring before him.

6) The Teacher catches his eye, and smiling at him, looks up at the smoke and claps her hands. The smoke suddenly disappears, along with everyone in the cavern. Nothing remains except for the fire and the black pool. Even the Teacher is gone.

# 38 ALIENATION (睽 KUI)

| | KUI Pictogram: | Meanings: |
|---|---|---|
| 睽 | Eyes 目 watching man shoot arrow 矢 (See Wieger, Lesson 112) | In opposition, separate, distant |

FIRE over LAKE: Clinging to Emotion

Natural: Lightning above the Lake
Outer Persona: Excited
Inner Spirit: Passionate
Element: Fire
Yang over Yin (Young Yang)

INNER ROOT GUA: #25 HEAVEN/THUNDER,
TRUTH
Yang over Yang (Old Yang)
Power Score = 7 (2nd Quartile)

## Scoring Matrix

| Gua Diagram | Line | Correctness | Activation | |
|---|---|---|---|---|
| | 6 | 0 | – | 0 |
| | 5 | 0 | | |
| | 4 | 0 | – | 0 |
| | 3 | 0 | | |
| | 2 | 0 | – | 0 |
| | 1 | 1 | | |

## Power Score: 2 (4th Quartile)

- Correctness: 1
- Activation: 0
- Carrying: 0
- Centrality: 1
- Reflection: 0

## Total Dual Score: 9 (3rd Quartile)

# 38 ALIENATION (睽 KUI)

"The Hidden Source" Narrative

Δ Δ

## Vision 18
### Through the Empty Worlds – The Witness
O
Alienation, clinging to emotion,
Rooted in Truth

1) The Witness hovers above a dark pool at the back of the cave. Muted greyed light flickers across its surface, reflecting light from a still burning fire. Suddenly he's pulled towards the pool and into its viscous depths.
2) While moving through the pool, he initially loses all sense of time and soon after that all sense of motion. He is lost in its empty black void. His sense of self momentarily disappears as well.
3) He soon finds himself not only moving again, but also once more possessed of spatial awareness. He floats within the center of a giant spherical chamber, as if he were a pinpoint of awareness within the hollow expanse of his own skull.
4) He now feels himself moving further outwards and upwards. He crosses what appears to be an enclosing wall, as the texture of the region changes abruptly. A section of the wall dissolves before him.
5) Hovering above the wall, he examines this open section and its well-defined architecture and structure. The wall itself is part of a curved shell enclosing an enormous black expanse.
6) The wall texture is sponge-like in nature. It has repeating patterns of thin walled hexagons, like a honeycombed beehive. Nothing is visible inside these hexagons, with the bulk of the wall's mass empty space. The color of their edges, as well as their insides, is black. When the light of his awareness passes over them, the edges light up with a dull grey.

# 39 HARDSHIP (蹇 JIAN)

| 蹇 | JIAN Pictogram:<br><br>Walled in 蹇 steps 足<br>(See Wieger, Lessons 47, 112) | Meanings:<br><br>Lame, crippled,<br>unfortunate,<br>difficult |
|---|---|---|

## WATER over MOUNTAIN: Darkness Bound

Natural: Fog covers the Mountain
Outer Persona: Immersed
Inner Spirit: Stubborn
Element: Water
Yin over Yang (Young Yin)

## INNER ROOT GUA: #46 EARTH/WIND, GROWING UPWARD
Yin over Yin (Old Yin)
Power Score = 6 (2nd Quartile)

### Scoring Matrix

| Gua Diagram | Line | Correctness | Activation | |
|---|---|---|---|---|
| | 6 | 1 | ★ | 2 |
| | 5 | 1 | | |
| | 4 | 1 | O | 1 |
| | 3 | 1 | | |
| | 2 | 1 | O | 1 |
| | 1 | 0 | | |

## Power Score: 12 (1st Quartile)
- Correctness: 5
- Activation: 4
- Carrying: 1
- Centrality: 2
- Reflection: 0

## Total Dual Score: 18 (1st Quartile)

# 39 HARDSHIP (蹇 JIAN)

"The Soul Revelation" Narrative

△ △ △ △

## Vision 48
### Behind the Raven Mask – The Seeker
4

Hardship, with darkness bound,
Rooted in Growing Upward

1) The Seeker is sitting in meditation. Slipping deeper into trance, he is still aware of himself and his situation. He sees the form of a head beginning to form in front of him, floating in space.

2) As the head comes into focus, he realizes that the face is not visible but instead concealed behind some type of a dark mask. The mask completely obscures the front of the head, so that no other features such as hair or skin color are visible. Even the ears are hidden.

3) The mask is painted a deep black and looks to be made of wood, with only a slight curvature to fit over the face.

4) It does not look comfortable, but ill fitting and stiff, something worn as part of an initiatory ritual or some other kind of ceremonial gathering where one's identity must be hidden.

5) The only openings it has are two holes for the eyes. The Seeker realizes with a start that the eyes do not look normal, but appear to be colored solid black, with no whites visible.

6) A pointed protuberance is present where the nose would be. The Seeker recognizes that it is a long black beak, and that he is looking at a mask of the Raven. He does not know whom or what the mask conceals or its purpose in doing so.

# 40 LIBERATION (解 JIE)

| | JIE Pictogram: | Meanings: |
|---|---|---|
| 解 | Ox's 牛 horn 角 cut with knife 刀 (See Wieger, Lesson 142) | Separate, break up, loosen |

## THUNDER over WATER: Arising from Darkness

Natural: Thundering River Rapids
Outer Persona: Aroused
Inner Spirit: Immersed
Element: Wood
Yang over Yin (Young Yang)

INNER ROOT GUA: #45 LAKE/EARTH,
GATHERING
Yin over Yin (Old Yin)
Power Score = 7 (2nd Quartile)

### Scoring Matrix

| Gua Diagram | Line | Correctness | Activation | |
|---|---|---|---|---|
| | 6 | 1 | – | 0 |
| | 5 | 0 | | |
| | 4 | 0 | – | 0 |
| | 3 | 0 | | |
| | 2 | 0 | – | 0 |
| | 1 | 0 | | |

## Power Score: 2 (4th Quartile)

- Correctness: 1
- Activation: 0
- Carrying: 0
- Centrality: 1
- Reflection: 0

## Total Dual Score: 9 (3rd Quartile)

# 40 LIBERATION (解 JIE)

"The Hidden Source" Narrative

△ △

## Vision 20
### Escaping the Dark Rift — The Witness
O
Liberation, arising from darkness,
Rooted in Gathering

1) The Witness moves underground through a dark tunnel. He perceives alternating areas of dark shadows and dim light moving past him, all rendered in shades of grey. The light is coming from some unseen source ahead of him.

2) Twisting and turning through gloomy channels, the oscillating patterns of light and dark come faster and faster, like on a speeding subway train. Suddenly, rounding a sharp corner, a small area of dim white light becomes visible in the distance.

3) The light's shape is not round. The closer he gets, the more rough and jagged it appears. The tunnel's exit is now visible, ahead and above him, opening into a brightly lit region.

4) He experiences a quick moment of discontinuity. He is in the jagged opening for only an instant, before shooting into the sky. He catches the briefest glimpses of the landscape rushing by in greens and browns. Soon he sees only a bright blue sky punctuated by fluffy white clouds.

5) He looks for the sun, for that is his goal. After the darkness, he longs for the pure light. But the sun is behind the clouds. Soon he is immersed inside a misty fog-like area of diffuse greyish white light. All color and features have completely vanished. He must be in the clouds.

6) He continues to move upwards, as the light grows brighter and brighter, trying to escape the clouds. The light remains rendered only in shades of hazy grey. He still hopes to see the clear unadulterated source of this light, but greys are all he finds.

# 41 DECREASING (損 SUN)

| 損 | SUN Pictogram:<br><br>Hand 手 holding vessel 具<br><br>with open mouth 口 | Meanings:<br><br>Lose, decrease |
|---|---|---|

## MOUNTAIN over LAKE: Blocked Emotion

Natural: Lake formed on side of Mountain
Outer Persona: Stubborn
Inner Spirit: Passionate
Element: Earth
Yang over Yin (Young Yang)

INNER ROOT GUA: #21 FIRE/THUNDER,
ERADICATING
Yang over Yang (Old Yang)
Power Score = 3 (4$^{th}$ Quartile)

### Scoring Matrix

| Gua Diagram | Line | Correctness | Activation | |
|---|---|---|---|---|
| | 6 | 0 | – | 0 |
| | 5 | 0 | | |
| | 4 | 1 | O | 1 |
| | 3 | 0 | | |
| | 2 | 0 | – | 0 |
| | 1 | 1 | | |

## Power Score: 4 (3rd Quartile)

- Correctness: 2
- Activation: 1
- Carrying: 0
- Centrality: 1
- Reflection: 0

## Total Dual Score: 7 (4th Quartile)

## 41 DECREASING (損 SUN)

"The Heavenly Revelation" Narrative

Δ

### Vision 57
### The Mundane Loses Its Influence – The Seeker
1
Decreasing, with blocked emotion,
Rooted in Eradicating

1) The Seeker is sitting in meditation in the transitional phase, his body numb and his breath slow and gentle. Slipping into deeper trance, he is still aware of himself and his situation. A scene begins to form, hanging in space before him.

2) He is floating above the ground, which is yellow-brown in color and sandy in texture. Covering its surface, he sees a series of grey-blue stones, flattened and smoothed as if burnished by flowing waters in a creek bed.

3) As he watches, the stones begin to wobble and vibrate, the result of some invisible force washing over them. They begin to slide across the ground, colliding and bouncing off each other. Their movements become increasingly more frenetic.

4) Finally, the stones, winning their battle against the forces that constrained them, quiet their frantic motions, and gently rise into the air. There, they settle into slow moving trajectories a couple of feet above the ground, as if they were floating on the surface of a smoothly undulating sea.

5) At this point the Seeker's gaze zooms towards a single stone. He notices some markings on the stone's grey surface.

6) Closer still, he sees a rectangular shaped window set into its rocky surface. Within the window, a bright blue sky is visible, with slowly floating white clouds.

## 42 INCREASING (益 YI)

| | YI Pictogram: | Meanings: |
|---|---|---|
| 益 | Water 水 overflowing<br><br>saucer 皿<br>(See Wieger, Lesson 125) | Benefit, increase |

### WIND over THUNDER: Penetrating Action

Natural: Trees amid new Growth
Outer Persona: Focused
Inner Spirit: Aroused
Element: Wood
Yin over Yang (Young Yin)

### INNER ROOT GUA: #22 MOUNTAIN/FIRE, ADORNMENT
Yang over Yang (Old Yang)
Power Score = 7 (2$^{nd}$ Quartile)

### Scoring Matrix

| Gua Diagram | Line | Correctness | Activation | |
|---|---|---|---|---|
| | 6 | 0 | – | 0 |
| | 5 | 1 | | |
| | 4 | 1 | O | 1 |
| | 3 | 0 | | |
| | 2 | 1 | ★ | 2 |
| | 1 | 1 | | |

### Power Score: 10 (1st Quartile)
- Correctness: 4
- Activation: 3
- Carrying: 1
- Centrality: 2
- Reflection: 0

### Total Dual Score: 17 (1st Quartile)

# 42 INCREASING (益 YI)

## "The Castle Redemption" Narrative

△ △ △ △

### Vision 29

#### Grant of the Golden Key – The Apprentice Smith

3

Increasing, with penetrating action,
Rooted in Adornment

1) The Apprentice Blacksmith is within the depths of the castle. He stands in a candle lit, furnished room on one of the castle's lower, heavily guarded floors. He doesn't know why he is here.

2) In walks a woman of regal bearing, wearing a long ornate white and lavender dress with a flowing headpiece. Looking closely at her face, he recognizes her as the Teacher.

3) She directs him to sit in a plain, squarish wooden chair, while she sits in an elaborately carved, high-backed, throne-like chair, facing him.

4) He sees that in her lap she is cradling an object wrapped in plush, violet colored, velvet cloth. She looks down at this object and then at him and smiles.

5) She peels back the cloth to show him what she is holding. It is an elaborately crafted skeleton key, about eight inches in length, made of solid gold that sparkles in the candle light.

6) She bows her head to him ever so subtly and hands him the key, which he receives in his two trembling, outstretched hands. He is surprised by its weight. He has no idea about whether the key is merely ceremonial or the solution to some locked door waiting for him in his future. He straps the key to his back.

## 43 BREAKING THROUGH (夬 GUAI)

| 夬 | GUAI Pictogram:<br><br>Hand 又 holding half an<br>object 中<br>(See Wieger, Lesson 43) | Meanings:<br><br>Parted, certain,<br>decisive |
|---|---|---|

### LAKE over HEAVEN: Joyful Advance

Natural: Sky reflected on Lake
Outer Persona: Passionate
Inner Spirit: Engaged
Element: Metal (Silver)
Yin over Yang (Young Yin)

INNER ROOT GUA: #43 LAKE/HEAVEN,
BREAKING THROUGH
Yin over Yang (Young Yin)
Power Score = 8 (2nd Quartile)

### Scoring Matrix

| Gua Diagram | Line | Correctness | Activation | |
|---|---|---|---|---|
| | 6 | 1 | ★ | 2 |
| | 5 | 1 | | |
| | 4 | 0 | – | 0 |
| | 3 | 1 | | |
| | 2 | 0 | – | 0 |
| | 1 | 1 | | |

### Power Score: 8 (2nd Quartile)

- Correctness: 4
- Activation: 2
- Carrying: 0
- Centrality: 2
- Reflection: 0

### Total Dual Score: 16 (1st Quartile)

# 43 BREAKING THROUGH (夬 GUAI)

"The Soul Revelation" Narrative

△ △ △ △

## Vision 51
### Shadow Communion – The Seeker
2
Breaking Through, with joyful advance,
Rooted in more Breaking Through

1) The Seeker is sitting in his room, meditating. Sinking deeper into trance, but still aware of himself and his situation, he sees a face and torso coming into focus, suspended in the shimmering space before him.
2) He recognizes the face as that of the Shadow Warrior, who he had previously confronted and bested in an earlier vision, leaving the Warrior immobilized on the ground.
3) As before, the Warrior is dressed in black leather armor, covered with silver studs and short spikes. His features are broad and coarse, his eyes dark, his black beard and hair full and tangled.
4) The Seeker examines the Warrior's features carefully, looking for some kind of clue about why he is seeing him again. The face remains impassive, though resolute in its gaze. The Warrior is looking straight ahead, as if to avoid eye contact with him.
5) The Seeker realizes he feels no animosity while looking at the Warrior, viewing him more as a fellow traveler than a hostile force. This feels like a revelation to him, and, as if in recognition of this, the Warrior suddenly shifts his gaze and looks directly at him.
6) As the Seeker watches, the Warrior's features begin to morph into someone else. He sees a younger version of his own face beginning to emerge.

# 44 ENCOUNTERING (姤 GOU)

| 姤 | GOU Pictogram:<br><br>Woman 女 sovereign 后<br>(See Wieger, Lesson 67) | Meanings:<br><br>Mate, copulate |
|---|---|---|

## HEAVEN over WIND: Power Entering

Natural: Wind blows beneath clear Skies
Outer Persona: Engaged
Inner Spirit: Focused
Element: Metal (Gold)
Yang over Yin (Young Yang)

INNER ROOT GUA: #44 HEAVEN/WIND,
ENCOUNTERING
Yang over Yin (Young Yin)
Power Score = 4 (3$^{rd}$ Quartile)

### Scoring Matrix

| Gua Diagram | Line | Correctness | Activation | |
|---|---|---|---|---|
| | 6 | 0 | – | 0 |
| | 5 | 1 | | |
| | 4 | 0 | – | 0 |
| | 3 | 1 | | |
| | 2 | 0 | – | 0 |
| | 1 | 0 | | |

## Power Score: 4 (3rd Quartile)

- Correctness: 2
- Activation: 0
- Carrying: 0
- Centrality: 2
- Reflection: 0

## Total Dual Score: 8 (4th Quartile)

# 44 ENCOUNTERING (姤 GOU)

"The Dragon Encounter" Narrative

Δ

## Vision 13
### Destiny Revealed – The Spirit Walker
O
Encountering, with power entering,
Rooted in more Encountering

1) Her son is right. She is not happy. That was the last thought Spirit Walker heard from her son's mind before her consciousness snapped back. Looking down the trail, she watches her son appear, trailed by a flock of panting children. He stops before her, shrugs, and starts to speak.

2) "Don't bother. I don't need any more of your stories," she said. "I know exactly what happened out there today." A puzzled look comes over First Son's face.

3) "Let me put it to you as simply as I can, First Son. If you weren't my eldest son and hadn't just had a birthday, today you and the other children would be dead. And not just you -- maybe even the whole village as well. I can't say it any plainer." First Son looks confused and a little scared.

4) "A dragon, really? The Spirit Father? Are you crazy? Remember the impulse that hit you when you picked up that rock, stopping you dead in your tracks? That was my doing. If I hadn't grabbed hold of you, you'd all be dragon chow by now. Spirit Father must be approached with respect and proper ritual."

5) "But that's not all. There is something else you need to know. Our family has certain capabilities that begin to appear when we hit eighteen years of age, as you did on the last full moon."

6) "Your nascent psychic capabilities are just now beginning to emerge. That means I can look inside your mind. I shared the experiences of your little misadventure by the swamp. Know that you have a destiny now. Time to grow up. Buckle down and learn to use your powers to serve your tribe."

# 45 GATHERING (萃 CUI)

| 萃 | CUI Pictogram:<br><br>Grass ⁺⁺ with servant 卒<br>(See Wieger, Lesson 16) | Meanings:<br><br>Collect, gather, dense |
|---|---|---|

## LAKE over EARTH: Joyful Received

Natural: Lake forms on the Earth
Outer Persona: Passionate
Inner Spirit: Yielding
Element: Metal (Silver)
Yin over Yin (Old Yin)

INNER ROOT GUA: #39 WATER/MOUNTAIN,
HARDSHIP
Yin over Yang (Young Yin)
Power Score = 12 (1ˢᵗ Quartile)

### Scoring Matrix

| Gua Diagram | Line | Correctness | Activation | |
|---|---|---|---|---|
| | 6 | 1 | O | 1 |
| | 5 | 1 | | |
| | 4 | 0 | – | 0 |
| | 3 | 0 | | |
| | 2 | 1 | O | 1 |
| | 1 | 0 | | |

## Power Score: 7 (2ⁿᵈ Quartile)

- Correctness: 3
- Activation: 2
- Carrying: 0
- Centrality: 2
- Reflection: 0

## Total Dual Score: 19 (1st Quartile)

# 45 GATHERING (萃 CUI)

"The Nexus Formation" Narrative

△ △ △ △

## Vision 4
### The Melding of Souls – The Traveller
2
Gathering, joyful receiving,
Rooted in Hardship

1) The Traveller is standing in a clearing in the woods. He watches as rows of children flow past him around a bend on a hiking path and then move away. The width of the path is narrow, only wide enough for one person at a time to walk along it.

2) As the scene comes more into focus, he realizes something strange is occurring. As the children round the corner, their growth suddenly accelerates, and they rapidly age before his eyes, from child to adult, from adult to elder. Some grow at different speeds than others.

3) At the same time as they age, the solidity and opacity of their bodies start to diminish and fade away. The faster they age, the more translucent their bodies become, until they are almost completely transparent, ghostlike in appearance.

4) Shifting his gaze behind him to get a better look at this phenomenon, he sees the path abruptly stop. At the end of the path stands a large translucent figure, the Nexus. Its form, continually fluctuating in shape, is hard for him to focus on.

5) As the transparent body of each individual gets close to the Nexus, it swells and reaches out to grab the walker, like the pseudopod of an amoeba reaching out for its prey. The shape of the walker distorts as well, as it is pulled in.

6) The shape of the Nexus temporarily morphs into the shape of the body it absorbs, before resuming its amorphous shape, cycling from one consumed shape to another, as an endless stream of figures dissolve into its figure-shaped vortex of pulsating energy.

## 46 GROWING UPWARD (升 SHENG)

| 升 | SHENG Pictogram:<br><br>Measuring 10 十 Ladles 勺<br>(See Wieger, Lesson 98) | Meanings:<br><br>To ascend, to rise up |
|---|---|---|

### EARTH over WIND: Receptive to Entry

Natural: Tree with deep roots in Earth
Outer Persona: Yielding
Inner Spirit: Focused
Element: Earth
Yin over Yin (Old Yin)

INNER ROOT GUA: #40 THUNDER/WATER,
LIBERATION
Yang over Yin (Young Yang)
Power Score = 2 (4th Quartile)

### Scoring Matrix

| Gua Diagram | Line | Correctness | Activation | |
|---|---|---|---|---|
| | 6 | 1 | O | 1 |
| | 5 | 0 | | |
| | 4 | 1 | O | 1 |
| | 3 | 1 | | |
| | 2 | 0 | – | 0 |
| | 1 | 0 | | |

### Power Score: 6 (2nd Quartile)

- Correctness: 3
- Activation: 2
- Carrying: 0
- Centrality: 1
- Reflection: 0

### Total Dual Score: 8 (4th Quartile)

# 46 GROWING UPWARD (升 SHENG)

"The Heavenly Revelation" Narrative

Δ

## Vision 60
### Climbing Heaven's Stairway – The Traveller

2

Growing Upward, receptive to entry,
Rooted in Liberation

1) The Traveller stands on ground enveloped in a swirling mist, looking at the bottom steps of a stairway that vanishes into the clouds. He knows his task is to climb these stairs.

2) The steps are formed of a pitted granite rock. They are larger than normal size, about two feet deep and high.

3) Beginning to climb the steps, the Traveller soon realizes how steep its ascent is. Glancing to the side, he is unable to determine the width of the steps, since all he sees is more mist.

4) Step by step he climbs, with the going made increasingly slower by the steep angle and size of each step. Soon he is leaning forward to use his hands and arms to help pull him to the next step. His face drawn close, he notices how worn and corroded the surface is.

5) The mist clears as he rises higher and higher. He now sees that the stairway is built into the side of a giant, multi-leveled pyramid, which grows steeper and steeper the higher it climbs.

6) Climbing still higher, the clouds pull back, and he is able to see a high-walled temple-like structure perched on the top of the pyramid, though it is still far in the distance. He also discovers that he is not alone on the stairway, as he sees a scattering of others struggling up the steps ahead of him, their progress even slower than his as the ascent becomes almost vertical.

# 47 EXHAUSTING (困 KUN)

| 困 | KUN Pictogram:<br><br>Tree 木 growing in<br><br>enclosure 口<br>(See Wieger, Lesson 119) | Meanings:<br><br>Surround, besiege,<br>difficult |
|---|---|---|

## LAKE over WATER: Sinking into Darkness

Natural: Water draining from Lake
Outer Persona: Passionate
Inner Spirit: Immersed
Element: Metal (Silver)
Yin over Yin (Old Yin)

INNER ROOT GUA: #31 LAKE/MOUNTAIN,
INFLUENCE
Yin over Yang (Young Yin)
Power Score = 9 (1$^{st}$ Quartile)

### Scoring Matrix

| Gua Diagram | Line | Correctness | Activation | |
|---|---|---|---|---|
| | 6 | 1 | O | 1 |
| | 5 | 1 | | |
| | 4 | 0 | – | 0 |
| | 3 | 0 | | |
| | 2 | 0 | – | 0 |
| | 1 | 0 | | |

## Power Score: 5 (3rd Quartile)

- Correctness: 2
- Activation: 1
- Carrying: 0
- Centrality: 2
- Reflection: 0

## Total Dual Score: 14 (2nd Quartile)

# 47 EXHAUSTING (困 KUN)

"The Soul Revelation" Narrative

△ △ △

## Vision 50
### The Return of the King – The Seeker
1

Exhausting, sinking into darkness,
Rooted in Influence

1) The Seeker is sitting in his room, meditating. Sinking deeper into trance, but still aware of himself and his situation, he sees the shape of a head beginning to form in front of him, hovering in space.

2) The head is male, with a long, narrow face and straight nose, framed by long, curly black hair down to his shoulders and a short beard with tight curls. Something about his appearance suggests to the Seeker that the individual is Greek.

3) The Greek looks back at the Seeker with recognition in his eyes. His expression indicates that he has encountered the Seeker before.

4) The Seeker stares back at the Greek, trying to identify where he might have seen him before. He remembers that he has seen the Greek not in the mundane world but in a vision, as the King served by the Apprentice Blacksmith.

5) The Greek, noting a glimmer of recognition in the Seeker's eyes, winks at him and begins to speak: "I am the King of Chaos and have been active throughout history."

6) For some reason, the name "Agamemnon" pops into the Seeker's mind. The Seeker wonders whether this being is the spreader of chaos or the source of order in a world beset by chaos.

# 48 REPLENISHING (井 JING)

| | JING Pictogram: | Meanings: |
|---|---|---|
| 井 | Field divided into lots with well at center (See Wieger, Lesson 115) | Well, mine, pit |

WATER over WIND: Streaming Penetration

Natural: Rain falling on Trees
Outer Persona: Immersed
Inner Spirit: Focused
Element: Water
Yin over Yin (Old Yin)

INNER ROOT GUA: #32 THUNDER/WIND,
PERSEVERANCE
Yang over Yin (Young Yang)
Power Score = 4 (3rd Quartile)

## Scoring Matrix

| Gua Diagram | Line | Correctness | Activation | |
|---|---|---|---|---|
| | 6 | 1 | ★ | 2 |
| | 5 | 1 | | |
| | 4 | 1 | O | 1 |
| | 3 | 1 | | |
| | 2 | 0 | – | 0 |
| | 1 | 0 | | |

## Power Score: 10 (1st Quartile)

- Correctness: 4
- Activation: 3
- Carrying: 1
- Centrality: 2
- Reflection: 0

## Total Dual Score: 14 (2nd Quartile)

# 48 REPLENISHING (井 JING)

"The Castle Redemption" Narrative

△ △ △

## Vision 28
## Empowering the King — The Apprentice Smith
3

Replenishing, with streaming penetration,
Rooted in Perseverance

1) The Apprentice Blacksmith is standing on the barren fields outside the castle walls. He burns with the Shadow Energy swirling inside him that he captured from the Shadow Warrior.

2) He turns and sees the King approaching him, alone and without the retinue of guards that normally accompany him.

3) More surprisingly, the King stops and kneels on one knee, beckoning him to come close. He approaches the King with hesitant steps, and stopping before him, bows his head in a sign of supplication.

4) He knows what the King expects him to do. The King looks up at him as he exhales the black vapors of the Shadow Energy directly into the King's open mouth. The King seems to grow in stature and vitality as he absorbs the freed vapors.

5) The next thing he knows, he and the King are standing on a rocky plain with the assembled forces of the Dark Army spread out before them. None of the King's army is present, only the two of them. The King tells him he is there only as witness.

6) What he witnesses is remarkable. Standing aside, he observes the ensuing battle, as the King sweeps through the attacking multitudes as if they were made of paper, rendering them literally into clouds of dust with swirling swords held in each of his hands.

# 49 REVOLUTION (MOLTING) (革 GE)

| 革 | GE Pictogram:<br>Raw skin of flayed sheep stretched out<br>(See Wieger, Lesson 105) | Meanings:<br>Leather, hides, remove |
|---|---|---|

## LAKE over FIRE: Joyful Consuming

Natural: Lightning reflected in Lake
Outer Persona: Passionate
Inner Spirit: Excited
Element: Metal (Silver)
Yin over Yang (Young Yin)

## INNER ROOT GUA: #5 WATER/HEAVEN, WAITING
Yin over Yang (Young Yin)
Power Score = 12 (1st Quartile)

### Scoring Matrix

| Gua Diagram | Line | Correctness | Activation | |
|---|---|---|---|---|
| | 6 | 1 | ★ | 2 |
| | 5 | 1 | | |
| | 4 | 0 | – | 0 |
| | 3 | 1 | | |
| | 2 | 1 | ★ | 2 |
| | 1 | 1 | | |

## Power Score: 11 (1st Quartile)

- Correctness: 5
- Activation: 4
- Carrying: 0
- Centrality: 2
- Reflection: 0

## Total Dual Score: 23 (1st Quartile)

# 49 REVOLUTION (MOLTING) (革 GE)

"The Soul Revelation" Narrative

△ △ △ △

## Vision 55
### The Soul Reversion – The Seeker
4
Revolution, a joyful consuming,
Rooted in Waiting

1) The Seeker is sitting in his room, meditating. Sinking deeper into trance, he is still aware of himself and his situation. A scene begins to form, hovering in space. But rather than appearing in front of him, it takes shape in the area to the left of where he sits.

2) He sees there an image of himself as a young man, the same 35 years of age that he appears as in so many other visions. Both head and upper torso are visible.

3) Suddenly, the image of him starts to pulse and throb, as if some force trapped within was trying to escape. Lines of fracture spread over its surface, which soon shatters into a collection of disjointed polygonal facets. These shapes vibrate and rotate and slide over one another, revealing themselves to be three-dimensional in nature.

4) As he watches, the entire body turns itself inside out, pieces from the inside flowing to the outside, morphing into new shapes and textures as the segments tumble over each other seeking their new destinations.

5) When the transformation is complete, an entirely new person is present. She is a woman, with long straight brown hair, a face that is a softer, feminized version of his original image, still 35 years of age.

6) The Seeker realizes that this woman is the female version of him, and more shockingly, that she is the Teacher.

# 50 THE CAULDRON (鼎 DING)

| | DING Pictogram: | Meanings: |
|---|---|---|
| 鼎 | Ancient cooking cauldron | Tripod, Cauldron |

FIRE over WIND: Flames Spreading

Natural: Fire burning Trees
Outer Persona: Excited
Inner Spirit: Focused
Element: Fire
Yang over Yin (Young Yang)

INNER ROOT GUA: #6 HEAVEN/WATER,
CONTENTION
Yang over Yin (Young Yang)
Power Score = 3 (4th Quartile)

## Scoring Matrix

| Gua Diagram | Line | Correctness | Activation | |
|---|---|---|---|---|
| | 6 | 0 | – | 0 |
| | 5 | 0 | | |
| | 4 | 0 | – | 0 |
| | 3 | 1 | | |
| | 2 | 0 | – | 0 |
| | 1 | 0 | | |

## Power Score: 2 (4th Quartile)

- Correctness: 1
- Activation: 0
- Carrying: 0
- Centrality: 1
- Reflection: 0

## Total Dual Score: 5 (4th Quartile)

# 50 THE CAULDRON (鼎 DING)

"The Nexus Formation" Narrative

Δ

## Vision 6
### The Fiery Gauntlet – The Seeker

O

The Cauldron, with flames spreading,
Rooted in Contention

1) The Seeker is sitting in his room, meditating. He is in the transitional phase of meditation, his body numb and his breathing slow and gentle.

2) Sinking deeper into trance, he is still aware of himself and his situation. A flat two-dimensional image of a series of four pine trees sitting on a ridge slowly comes into focus. The four trees are spaced equally apart, spread out just enough that no tree overlaps with the branches of its neighbors.

3) The trees are a rich, highly saturated forest green in color. The sky behind them appears whitish grey. There are no visible shadows in the scene. Initially the scene is completely static. Nothing is moving. The air is still.

4) Soon the air around the trees begins to shimmer and vibrate. The flickering air around the trees starts to glow a bright translucent green, completely enveloping the branches and foliage of the trees. The trees are still visible through the bright glare of these dancing flame-shaped phantasms.

5) The trees are on fire, but they are not being consumed. There is no smoke. The flames are not the normal yellow orange red of a burning tree, but are a semi-transparent, bright shade of chartreuse green.

6) Suddenly the view zooms towards the flaming trees, which take up more and more of the image. Soon, passing through the branches of a tree, only the flames themselves are visible. Then the scene transforms again. All that remains is a solid expanse of bright translucent chartreuse.

# 51 TAKING ACTION (震 ZHEN)

| 震 | ZHEN Pictogram:<br><br>Rain 雨 in early<br>morning 辰 | Meanings:<br><br>Shake, tremor,<br>excite |
|---|---|---|

### THUNDER over THUNDER: Driven to Rise

Natural: Explosive Thunder
Outer Persona: Aroused
Inner Spirit: Aroused
Element: Wood
Yang over Yang (Old Yang)

INNER ROOT GUA: #3 WATER/THUNDER,
SPROUTING
Yin over Yang (Young Yin)
Power Score = 12 (1$^{st}$ Quartile)

### Scoring Matrix

| Gua Diagram | Line | Correctness | Activation | |
|---|---|---|---|---|
| | 6 | 1 | – | 0 |
| | 5 | 0 | | |
| | 4 | 0 | – | 0 |
| | 3 | 0 | | |
| | 2 | 1 | O | 1 |
| | 1 | 1 | | |

## Power Score: 4 (3rd Quartile)

- Correctness:  3
- Activation:  1
- Carrying:  0
- Centrality:  0
- Reflection:  0

## Total Dual Score: 16 (2nd Quartile)

## 51 TAKING ACTION (震 ZHEN)

"The Spirit Incursion" Narrative

Δ Δ Δ

### Vision 42
### Explosion's Echo – The Seeker
1

Taking Action, driven to rise,
Rooted in Beginning

1) The Seeker is sitting in his room meditating, deep in trance, lost in a state of deep, empty absence.
2) Within this empty state, something calls to him, igniting a spark that gives rise to a tiny kernel of consciousness.
3) As more of his senses return to him, he hears, seemingly in the distance, a deep rumbling roar.
4) Then, suddenly snapping back to full consciousness in the mundane world, he is rocked by thunderous waves of explosive sound.
5) The room itself seems to shake, and he would be tempted to believe that lightening had struck nearby, except that he sees that it is a perfectly clear, sunlit morning outside.
6) After about 5 more seconds of violent sound, the explosive echoes fade away, to be replaced by the normal sounds of the morning. No events within his immediate environment can account for what roused him so precipitously from his meditation.

# 52 KEEPING STILL (艮 GEN)

| | GEN Pictogram: | Meanings: |
|---|---|---|
| 艮 | Turn around 匕 and look in the eye 目 (See Wieger, Lesson 26) | Hard, obstinate |

## MOUNTAIN over MOUNTAIN: Bound by Tranquility

Natural: High Mountain Peaks
Outer Persona: Stubborn
Inner Spirit: Stubborn
Element: Earth
Yang over Yang (Old Yang)

INNER ROOT GUA: #4 MOUNTAIN/WATER,
CHILDHOOD
Yang over Yin (Young Yang)
Power Score = 2 (4th Quartile)

### Scoring Matrix

| Gua Diagram | Line | Correctness | Activation | |
|---|---|---|---|---|
| | 6 | 0 | – | 0 |
| | 5 | 0 | | |
| | 4 | 1 | O | 1 |
| | 3 | 1 | | |
| | 2 | 1 | – | 0 |
| | 1 | 0 | | |

## Power Score: 4 (3rd Quartile)

- Correctness: 3
- Activation: 1
- Carrying: 0
- Centrality: 0
- Reflection: 0

## Total Dual Score: 6 (4th Quartile)

## 52 KEEPING STILL (艮 GEN)

"The Spirit Incursion" Narrative

Δ

### Vision 43
### In the Arms of the Titan – The Seeker

1

Keeping Still, bound by tranquility,
Rooted in Childhood

1) The Seeker is sitting in his room, meditating. Sinking deeper into trance, he is still aware of himself and his situation. He suddenly feels that he is not alone in his room, as he senses a nearby presence.

2) The sensation of another presence grows even stronger until he feels that this entity is right in front of him. He feels a large mass looming over him.

3) He sits very still, unsure about what is happening around him, but not wanting to reveal his awareness of its presence.

4) Though his eyes are closed, he sees an image superimposed upon the dark field visible behind his closed eyelids. It is the translucent, shimmering shape of a large, hulking humanoid form, with spread arms moving to encircle him.

5) At the same time he feels, as an energetic force against his body, the presence of two large hands on his upper back. Their presence seems benevolent to him, as if he is being sheltered and protected by the entity leaning over him, though from what he does not know.

6) Although he is unable to make out any of the distinguishing features of this entity, since he experiences it only as an energetic pressure and afterimage behind his closed eyes, he somehow knows who it is. It is the Shadow Warrior, returned from an earlier vision of the Apprentice Blacksmith.

# 53 DEVELOP GRADUALLY (漸 JIAN)

| 漸 | JIAN Pictogram:<br>Water 氵 and cutting 斩<br>(cart with ax)<br>(See Wieger, Lesson 128) | Meanings:<br>Gradually |
|---|---|---|

### WIND over MOUNTAIN: Spreading Tranquility

Natural: Trees growing on Mountainside
Outer Persona: Focused
Inner Spirit: Stubborn
Element: Wood
Yin over Yang (Young Yin)

### INNER ROOT GUA: #18 MOUNTAIN/WIND, POISON (REMEDY)
Yang over Yin (Young Yin)
Power Score = 4 (3rd Quartile)

### Scoring Matrix

| Gua Diagram | Line | Correctness | Activation | |
|---|---|---|---|---|
| | 6 | 0 | – | 0 |
| | 5 | 1 | | |
| | 4 | 1 | O | 1 |
| | 3 | 1 | | |
| | 2 | 1 | O | 1 |
| | 1 | 0 | | |

### Power Score: 9 (1st Quartile)
- Correctness: 4
- Activation: 2
- Carrying: 1
- Centrality: 2
- Reflection: 0

### Total Dual Score: 13 (2nd Quartile)

# 53 DEVELOP GRADUALLY (漸 JIAN)

"The Hidden Source" Narrative

△ △ △

Vision 22

## The Tree of Worlds – The Witness

2

Developing Gradually, with spreading tranquility,
Rooted in Remedy

1) The Witness is in a forest glen, before a grove of trees. A particular tree in the center of the scene catches his attention. Then, everything disappears except for this single tree, suspended in a field of diffuse mist.

2) As he watches, the tree begins to change. Its features coalesce, losing their details. He now sees a flattened two-dimensional, skeletal rendering of a tree-shaped exemplar. All its leaves disappear.

3) New spherical shaped leaves begin to appear, brown, semi-translucent tokens that dangle like ornaments from the tree's twisting branches. The tree continues to change, slowly growing in girth and in height. The leaves also grow in diameter, though faster than the tree.

4) Where before the canopy of leaves was a pale brown, a rich bouquet of bright colors now blooms, spanning all colors of the rainbow. Continuing to grow in richness and brightness, the leaves glow with their own internal source of colored light.

5) The shape of the leaves also becomes more three-dimensional. They have doubled in size and are shaped like square-edged glass lenses, serving as windows for peering into other worlds.

6) Even though the leaves are glowing orbs of light, the body of the tree and its branches are still monochromic and flat, creating a stark contrast between the dark tree and its colorful crown of spectral fruit.

# 54 DOMESTICATED MAIDEN (歸妹 GUI MEI)

| 歸妹 | GUI MEI Pictogram:<br><br>Maiden 妹 arriving 止 with<br>a wife's broom 婦<br>(See Wieger, Lesson 44) | Meanings:<br><br>Marrying<br>Maiden |
|---|---|---|

## THUNDER over LAKE: Aroused by Passion

Natural: New growth rising on the Lake
Outer Persona: Aroused
Inner Spirit: Passionate
Element: Wood
Yang over Yin (Young Yang)

INNER ROOT GUA: #17 LAKE/THUNDER,
FOLLOWING
Yin over Yang (Young Yin)
Power Score = 9 (1st Quartile)

### Scoring Matrix

| Gua Diagram | Line | Correctness | Activation | |
|---|---|---|---|---|
| | 6 | 1 | – | 0 |
| | 5 | 0 | | |
| | 4 | 0 | – | 0 |
| | 3 | 0 | | |
| | 2 | 0 | – | 0 |
| | 1 | 1 | | |

## Power Score: 3 (4th Quartile)

- Correctness: 2
- Activation: 0
- Carrying: 0
- Centrality: 1
- Reflection: 0

## Total Dual Score: 12 (3rd Quartile)

## 54 DOMESTICATED MAIDEN (歸妹 GUI MEI)

"The Soul Revelation" Narrative

Δ Δ

### Vision 52
### Necklace of the Spirit Walker – The Seeker

O

Domesticated Maiden, aroused by passion,
Rooted in Following

1) The Seeker is sitting in his room, meditating. Sinking deeper into trance, he is still aware of himself and his situation. He views a face coming into focus, suspended before him.

2) He sees the face of a noble African woman, with smooth, chocolate-colored skin and very short black hair. She is staring straight ahead and is perfectly still. He recognizes this figure as the Spirit Walker from the First Son visions.

3) As more of the scene comes into view, he focuses on the woman's now visible shoulders and the top part of her torso. Her shoulders are bare, with the exception of a necklace draped across her shoulders, with vertical rows of beads hanging down that cover her chest.

4) The beads are cylindrical in shape, stacked on top of each other. There are six beads on each string.

5) The beads alternate in distinctive patterns of white and turquoise blue beads, with the same pattern present on all of the strings.

6) The overall effect of these patterns is a series of six blue and white horizontal rows draped across her chest in a distinctive pattern, which from the top reads white blue, white blue, white blue.

## 55 ABUNDANCE (豐 FENG)

| 豐 | FENG Pictogram:<br><br>Beans in a vessel 豆<br>(See Wieger, Lesson 97) | Meanings:<br><br>Abundant, lush,<br>plenty |
|---|---|---|

THUNDER over FIRE: Aroused by Illumination

Natural: Thunder echoes over Lightning
Outer Persona: Aroused
Inner Spirit: Excited
Element: Wood
Yang over Yang (Old Yang)

INNER ROOT GUA: #60 WATER/LAKE,
CONTAINMENT
Yin over Yin (Old Yin)
Power Score = 9 (1$^{st}$ Quartile)

### Scoring Matrix

| Gua Diagram | Line | Correctness | Activation | |
|---|---|---|---|---|
| | 6 | 1 | O | 1 |
| | 5 | 0 | | |
| | 4 | 0 | – | 0 |
| | 3 | 1 | | |
| | 2 | 1 | O | 1 |
| | 1 | 1 | | |

### Power Score: 6 (2$^{nd}$ Quartile)

- Correctness: 4
- Activation: 2
- Carrying: 0
- Centrality: 0
- Reflection: 0

## Total Dual Score: 15 (2nd Quartile)

## 55 ABUNDANCE (豐 FENG)

"The Face of the Deep" Narrative

△ △ △

### Vision 8
### <u>Swimming in Heaven's Light – The Rider</u>
2
Abundance, aroused by illumination,
Rooted in Containment

1) The Rider is deep under the sea. The waters are warm and welcoming, caressed by slow moving tropical currents.

2) Although he is far below the surface, the waters are translucent and clear, illuminated by shafts of shimmering light penetrating into their depths. The glistening image of the sun, though suspended high in the heavens, floats as a fuzzy sphere on its surface.

3) The waters reflect the colors of the warm sunlit sky and are a luminous greenish blue. Softly undulating wave-like mounds roll across its surface.

4) The Rider realizes that he is in the body of sea creature, with a long body and neck, and wings on its back that propel it through the waters and a tail that it uses to steer.

5) He rejoices in his newly found freedom, swimming and frolicking, making loops and figure eights in the receptive waters. Even though submerged, he feels as if he is flying.

6) His movements express the joy and freedom he is experiencing. He feels content and perfectly at home as he slices and darts up and down and left and right through the waters. He has no thoughts or memories but only the pure joy brought on by swimming. Ultimately he begins a set of lazy spirals that take him deeper and deeper into the warm soothing depths.

## 56 THE WANDERER (旅 LU)

| | LU Pictogram: | Meanings: |
|---|---|---|
| 旅 | People 氏 under flags<br>flying 扒<br>(See Wieger, Lesson 117) | Trip, journey, traveler |

FIRE over MOUNTAIN: Inflamed by Obstruction

Natural: Sun setting over Mountain
Outer Persona: Excited
Inner Spirit: Stubborn
Element: Fire
Yang over Yang (Old Yang)

INNER ROOT GUA: #59 WIND/WATER,
DISPERSING
Yin over Yin (Old Yin)
Power Score = 5 (3$^{rd}$ Quartile)

### Scoring Matrix

| Gua Diagram | Line | Correctness | Activation | |
|---|---|---|---|---|
| | 6 | 0 | – | 0 |
| | 5 | 0 | | |
| | 4 | 0 | – | 0 |
| | 3 | 1 | | |
| | 2 | 1 | – | 0 |
| | 1 | 0 | | |

## Power Score: 2 (4th Quartile)

- Correctness: 2
- Activation: 0
- Carrying: 0
- Centrality: 0
- Reflection: 0

## Total Dual Score: 7 (4th Quartile)

## 56 THE WANDERER (旅 LU)

"The Pyramid Ascension" Narrative

Δ

### Vision 36

### Climbing the White Tower – The Journeyman

O

The Wanderer, inflamed by obstruction,
Rooted in Dispersing

1) The Journeyman is on the ground floor of a towering structure. Looking about, he does not see any exit or doors. He does not know where he is.

2) The walls of the structure, which appear metallic in composition, are curved, giving it a cylindrical shape. Gazing up, he sees that the tower's central area is open. There are no solid floors spanning the tower beyond the one on which he stands.

3) Everything within the tower is colored a stark white, except for the silver colored railing that runs along the outer side of the walkways. He sees no furnishings or objects of any kind that break up the monotony of the tower's sterile environment or provide any clues about its purpose.

4) He begins to climb the walkways that spiral up the inside walls of the tower, always looking for some sign of other people, as well as a way to get out. But he sees no evidence of other people or any doors or windows.

5) Periodically, he comes across balcony platforms that are suspended out from the walkways, accessible by stairs. He dutifully climbs each one he encounters, looking for clues to the reason for his presence in this tower. But there is nothing to see.

6) He climbs and he climbs. As he nears the top, he discovers that there is a glass-enclosed structure suspended from the roof. He quickens his pace and heads for it.

## 57 PROCEEDING HUMBLY (巽 XUN)

| 巽 | XUN Pictogram:<br><br>Two seals 己 on table 共<br>(See Wieger, Lesson 55) | Meanings:<br>To elect, to<br>choose, to commit<br>to those chosen;<br>Obedient, modest |
|---|---|---|

### WIND over WIND: Focus Dispersed

Natural: Spreading Wings
Outer Persona: Focused
Inner Spirit: Focused
Element: Wood
Yin over Yin (Old Yin)

INNER ROOT GUA: #50 FIRE/WIND,
THE CAULDRON
Yang over Yin (Young Yang)
Power Score = 2 (4<sup>th</sup> Quartile)

### Scoring Matrix

| Gua Diagram | Line | Correctness | Activation | |
|---|---|---|---|---|
| | 6 | 0 | – | 0 |
| | 5 | 1 | | |
| | 4 | 1 | O | 1 |
| | 3 | 1 | | |
| | 2 | 0 | – | 0 |
| | 1 | 0 | | |

### Power Score: 7 (2<sup>nd</sup> Quartile)

- Correctness:  3
- Activation:  1
- Carrying:  1
- Centrality:  2
- Reflection:  0

### Total Dual Score: 9 (3<sup>rd</sup> Quartile)

# 57 PROCEEDING HUMBLY (巽 XUN)

"The Spirit Incursion" Narrative

Δ Δ

## Vision 41
## The Spirit Wings Unfold – The Seeker
1

Proceeding Humbly, with focus dispersed,
Rooted in the Cauldron

1) The Seeker is sitting in his room, meditating. As he starts to slip into a deeper trance, a loud, high pitched shriek abruptly snaps him back into his physical body. The sound reminded him of the shrill cry of a bird of prey.

2) At the same time, he feels his spine being ripped into three pieces down its vertical axis, one piece pulled to the right and the other to the left. Maybe the sound he heard was this rip.

3) Where before there had been one channel, he now feels three, the original central channel of the spinal column and two new auxiliary channels, one on each side.

4) He feels warm, vibrant energy spiraling up the central channel from a seemingly endless reservoir in his lower torso, where exiting the crown of his head, it begins to circulate in the shape of a halo above his head.

5) At the same time, subtle energy flows stream directly up the two side channels and exit next to each shoulder. Each column curves up and out past his ears before flowing back down in a oval shaped stream to the base of the spine to re-enter its original side channel.

6) The two distinct energy flows trace out the shape of wings on each side of his body. He feels like he has emerged from a cocoon and been reborn with a new etheric body.

## 58 JOYFUL (兑 DUI)

| 兑 | DUI Pictogram:<br><br>Person with open mouth 兄<br>(See Wieger, Lesson 29) | Meanings:<br><br>To speak, rejoice<br>(Modern: cash) |
|---|---|---|

### LAKE over LAKE: Deep Passion

Natural: Deep, still Lake
Outer Persona: Passionate
Inner Spirit: Passionate
Element: Metal (Silver)
Yin over Yin (Old Yin)

INNER ROOT GUA: #49 LAKE/FIRE,
REVOLUTION (MOLTING)
Yin over Yang (Young Yin)
Power Score = 11 (1st Quartile)

### Scoring Matrix

| Gua Diagram | Line | Correctness | Activation | |
|---|---|---|---|---|
| | 6 | 1 | O | 1 |
| | 5 | 1 | | |
| | 4 | 0 | – | 0 |
| | 3 | 0 | | |
| | 2 | 0 | – | 0 |
| | 1 | 1 | | |

## Power Score: 6 (2nd Quartile)

- Correctness: 3
- Activation: 1
- Carrying: 0
- Centrality: 2
- Reflection: 0

## Total Dual Score: 17 (1st Quartile)

# 58 JOYFUL (兑 DUI)

## "The Spirit Incursion" Narrative

△ △ △ △

### Vision 46
### Play of the White Tiger – The Seeker

1

Joyfulness, with its deep passion,
Rooted in Revolution

1) The Seeker is walking out in the mundane world, crossing the small bridge that spans the stream behind his house, accompanied by his wife.

2) He begins to climb the three sections of steps that lead up a small hill to a grassy area that overlooks the pond far below. The steps are old railroad ties set into the side of a dirt-covered path.

3) The ascending steps are in a zigzag configuration, with the first and third legs heading straight up the hill and the second leg cutting sharply across the hill at almost a 90-degree angle to the other two.

4) The Seeker, turning to his left, starts up the second leg. At the end of this leg there is a banked area on the side of the hill with a small, flattened area at its top. Looking up the steps he's about to climb, he sees a quick flash of movement in this area.

5) He believes a white animal head has just popped up and down. As he watches, it does this a couple more times. He recognizes it as the head of a cat, one much larger than a housecat. He asks his wife if she had seen the animal.

6) The cat's head peers at him one more time; its white paws are perched to the side to prop it up. He quickly climbs to the top of the steps to examine the area where he saw the cat. He sees no signs of it and realizes that the topography of the area made what he had just seen impossible.

# 59 DISPERSING (涣 HUAN)

| 涣 | HUAN Pictogram:<br><br>Wide, vast 奂 waters 氵 | Meanings:<br><br>Disperse, scatter |
|---|---|---|

## WIND over WATER: Spread into Darkness

Natural: Wings spread over the Waters
Outer Persona: Focused
Inner Spirit: Immersed
Element: Wood
Yin over Yin (Old Yin)

## INNER ROOT GUA: #56 FIRE/MOUNTAIN, THE WANDERER
Yang over Yang (Old Yang)
Power Score = 2 (4$^{th}$ Quartile)

### Scoring Matrix

| Gua Diagram | Line | Correctness | Activation | |
|---|---|---|---|---|
| | 6 | 0 | – | 0 |
| | 5 | 1 | | |
| | 4 | 1 | – | 0 |
| | 3 | 0 | | |
| | 2 | 0 | – | 0 |
| | 1 | 0 | | |

## Power Score: 5 (3rd Quartile)
- Correctness: 2
- Activation: 0
- Carrying: 1
- Centrality: 2
- Reflection: 0

## Total Dual Score: 7 (4th Quartile)

# 59 DISPERSING (渙 HUAN)

"The Face of the Deep" Narrative

Δ

## Vision 7
## Hovering over Stormy Seas — The Rider

O

Dispersing, spread into darkness,
Rooted in Wandering

1) The Rider sees dark, broiling clouds sweeping across a troubled sky. Below him an angry sea throbs and thrashes. The Rider is suspended in the midst of this boiling cauldron, buffeted by heavy winds and blowing foam.

2) Only his large wingspan keeps him airborne, as he hovers unsteadily above the waters. He feels his head held aloft on a long muscled neck and body, his four legs hugged tightly to his sides, his tail trying to keep him balanced. He knows himself as the Dragon.

3) The ocean rises up before him at a 45-degree angle. The seas are slate blue with the darkest elements almost black. The waves are not rounded or rolling. There are no curves to be seen.

4) Instead, jagged edges are all he sees, the waves like the teeth of some ravenous maw trying to consume him and the blowing foam the frothing saliva of some rabid beast. The waves lash out towards him, trying to pull him into the dark depths below.

5) In spite of the elemental violence of his surroundings, he feels no fear or peril or any emotion at all. He doesn't know why he is here, but he still tries to take in as many details as he can.

6) At this point he feels himself pulled toward the surface of the slashing waves. He goes into a steep dive, waves growing closer and closer as he plummets downwards in a tight spiral.

# 60 CONTAINMENT (節 JIE)

| 節 | JIE Pictogram:<br><br>Section 节 bamboo 竹<br>(See Wieger, Lesson 26) | Meanings:<br><br>Section,<br>temperate, part |
|---|---|---|

## WATER over LAKE: Swimming in the Deep

Natural: Fog formed over Lake
Outer Persona: Immersed
Inner Spirit: Passionate
Element: Water
Yin over Yin (Old Yin)

INNER ROOT GUA: #55 THUNDER/FIRE,
ABUNDANCE
Yang over Yang (Old Yang)
Power Score = 6 (2nd Quartile)

## Scoring Matrix

| Gua Diagram | Line | Correctness | Activation | |
|---|---|---|---|---|
| | 6 | 1 | O | 1 |
| | 5 | 1 | | |
| | 4 | 1 | O | 1 |
| | 3 | 0 | | |
| | 2 | 0 | – | 0 |
| | 1 | 1 | | |

## Power Score: 9 (1st Quartile)

- Correctness: 4
- Activation: 2
- Carrying: 1
- Centrality: 2
- Reflection: 0

## Total Dual Score: 15 (2nd Quartile)

# 60 CONTAINMENT (節 JIE)

"The Hidden Source" Narrative

△ △ △

Vision 19

## Gorge of the Crystal River – The Witness

2

Containment, swimming in the deep,
Rooted in Abundance

1) The Witness is deep underground, with jagged stonewalls pressing on him. His awareness is initially fixed, focused on an area immediately above him, towards his right.

2) He soon is moving forward, propelled at a steady pace through a twisting, cavern-like tunnel that cuts through the mountain around him.

3) Everything is dark except for a narrow sphere of golden illumination shining out from the center of his awareness. Passing close by, he sees craggy protuberances covered with regions of crystalline facets and reflective gold, bouncing the light in a multitude of directions, dazzling his awareness with a fireworks-like display of brightly lit, glistening golden hues.

4) Looking down, he is following the meandering path of a deep crevasse winding its way through the mountain, carved out by the waters of a cascading, rapidly flowing river.

5) The river, illuminated by the light of his awareness, is a surprisingly rich shade of blue, even though there is no sky above for it to reflect. Foamy areas of the river reflect the bright golden color of the light from above.

6) The river is moving in the same direction as he is but at a greater velocity. He studies the different patterns of its flow that gyrate beneath him as he tunnels through the mountain's interiors.

## 61 INNER TRUTH (中孚 ZHONG FU)

| 中孚 | ZHONG FU Pictogram: Inner 中 claws ⌐ over offspring 子 (confidence) (See Wieger, Lesson94) | Meanings: ZHONG: Inner FU: Trust, confidence |
|---|---|---|

### WIND over LAKE: Penetrating into the Deep

Natural: Wings spread over a Lake
Outer Persona: Focused
Inner Spirit: Passionate
Element: Wood
Yin over Yin (Old Yin)

INNER ROOT GUA: #30 FIRE/FIRE,
FIRE
Yang over Yang (Old Yang)
Power Score = 5 (3$^{rd}$ Quartile)

### Scoring Matrix

| Gua Diagram | Line | Correctness | Activation | |
|---|---|---|---|---|
| | 6 | 0 | – | 0 |
| | 5 | 1 | | |
| | 4 | 1 | O | 1 |
| | 3 | 0 | | |
| | 2 | 0 | – | 0 |
| | 1 | 1 | | |

### Power Score: 8 (2nd Quartile)

- Correctness: 3
- Activation: 1
- Carrying: 1
- Centrality: 2
- Reflection: 1

### Total Dual Score: 13 (2nd Quartile)

# 61 INNER TRUTH (中孚 ZHONG FU)

"The Dragon Encounter" Narrative

Δ Δ Δ

## Vision 14
## In The Well of Souls – The Rider
1
Inner Truth, penetrating into the deep,
Rooted in Fire

1) The Rider is suspended within the walls of a giant, cylindrically shaped chamber. He is surrounded on all sides by striated, sandy colored cliffs, whose scope is so enormous that he is only able to see a small segment of them at a time.

2) Twisting his long neck to look around him, he cannot see the top or bottom edges of the cavern. His long body is suspended on giant reptilian wings, held aloft by a gentle but persistent warm updraft. He flies once more as the Dragon.

3) While floating there, he has no thoughts, no sense of identity, no memories of having been there before.

4) As more of the scene comes into focus, he realizes the cliff walls are not solid but are punctuated by a scattered series of small dark recessions. His field of view suddenly zooms in on an area to his right containing several of these recessed features.

5) He sees now these are actually small caves set into the sides of the cliffs, big enough to contain only a single individual. Some caves are close together and others isolated and far apart.

6) As he gets closer still he sees the caves are not empty. Each cave contains a solitary individual sitting cross-legged in its mouth. The individuals are both men and women, dressed in a wide variety of different garments, some primitive and others more contemporary.

# 62 SMALL CROSSING (小過 XIAO GUO)

| 小過 | XIAO GUO Pictogram:<br><br>Small 小 moving 辵<br>with phonetic | Meanings:<br><br>Small crossing, passing |
|---|---|---|

### THUNDER over MOUNTAIN: Aroused from Stillness

Natural: New growth on the Mountain
Outer Persona: Aroused
Inner Spirit: Stubborn
Element: Wood
Yang over Yang (Old Yang)

INNER ROOT GUA: #29 WATER/WATER,
THE PIT (DARKNESS)
Yin over Yin (Old Yin)
Power Score = 8 (2nd Quartile)

### Scoring Matrix

| Gua Diagram | Line | Correctness | Activation | |
|---|---|---|---|---|
| | 6 | 1 | O | 1 |
| | 5 | 0 | | |
| | 4 | 0 | – | 0 |
| | 3 | 1 | | |
| | 2 | 1 | – | 0 |
| | 1 | 0 | | |

## Power Score: 5 (3rd Quartile)

- Correctness:  3
- Activation:  1
- Carrying:  0
- Centrality:  0
- Reflection:  1

## Total Dual Score: 13 (2nd Quartile)

# 62 SMALL CROSSING (小過 XIAO GUO)

"The Castle Redemption" Narrative

## Δ Δ Δ

### Vision 26
### Called to the King's Service – The Apprentice Smith

1

Small Crossing, aroused from stillness,
Rooted in Darkness

1) The Apprentice Blacksmith enters the castle, immersed in the crowd of people fleeing the village, pushing and shoving in a frantic attempt to enter before the gates are closed.

2) A short time later the Apprentice finds himself in a small chamber. Puzzled about where he is, he runs his hand over the rough square blocks of granite making up the wall before him, only inches from his face.

3) Looking around, the Apprentice realizes he is alone in the darkened room. He has no idea about why he is here.

4) As more of his senses return to him, he feels a weight pressing down on his back and shoulders. He discovers that he is wearing a shirt of grey rusty chainmail over his everyday clothes.

5) Looking down at his chest, he sees that a soiled white tunic covers the chainmail, cinched with a rope for a belt. It has a large blue square in its center, with a strange looking coat-of-arms he does not recognize engraved on it. Its bottom half is shaped like an upturned horseshoe, with each end topped by an oval shape. A shaft runs up its center with a diamond shape at its top.

6) Turning behind him, he realizes a door has opened, casting light into the small alcove in which he stands, revealing a view of a rocky plain outside the walls.

# 63 ALREADY ACROSS (既濟 JI JI)

| 既濟 | JI JI Pictogram:<br>Already 既 waters 氵<br>arranged 齊<br>(See Wieger, Lesson 174) | Meanings:<br><br>Ji: already<br>Ji: ferried |
|---|---|---|

### WATER over FIRE: Streaming with Illumination

Natural: Boiling Water, Rising Steam
Outer Persona: Immersed
Inner Spirit: Excited
Element: Water
Yin over Yang (Young Yin)

INNER ROOT GUA: #11 EARTH/HEAVEN,
ADVANCE
Yin over Yang (Young Yin)
Power Score = 8 (2nd Quartile)

### Scoring Matrix

| Gua Diagram | Line | Correctness | Activation | |
|---|---|---|---|---|
| | 6 | 1 | ★ | 2 |
| | 5 | 1 | | |
| | 4 | 1 | ★ | 2 |
| | 3 | 1 | | |
| | 2 | 1 | ★ | 2 |
| | 1 | 1 | | |

## Power Score: 15 (1st Quartile)

- Correctness: 6
- Activation: 6
- Carrying: 1
- Centrality: 2
- Reflection: 0

## Total Dual Score: 23 (1st Quartile)

# 63 ALREADY ACROSS (既濟 JI JI)

"The Heavenly Revelation" Narrative

△ △ △ △

Vision 63

## Soul's Nexus Complete – The Witness
6

Already Across, streaming with illumination,
Rooted in Advance

1) Floating against a deep black background, the Witness sees a vast field of sparkling, multicolored stars.

2) He soon finds himself in the midst of these objects. Moving closer to them, as they float around him, he sees that they are not stars, but glowing, colored, translucent orbs.

3) He realizes that he has seen these glass-like globes before, though he is not immediately able to remember when or where. He then recalls that these same orbs were on the World Tree of an earlier vision.

4) As he watches, lines of glowing force stream out from all the globes, connecting them immediately with all the adjacent ones, and later with all the others as well. The result is a shimmering, web-like network of crisscrossing lines of energy, with all the globes glowing at the connection points.

5) He is now within this giant mesh network of completely connected nodes. Pulling further back, he sees that the overall network is in the shape of a giant 3-D structure composed of layers of concentric spheres.

6) In the center of this structure he discovers the presence of a golden, sun-like throbbing sphere. He watches as more and more of the surrounding network begins to be pulled towards the central sphere, which grows ever larger as it absorbs their energies. His feels himself starting to move as well, as he is caught up in the space collapsing around him.

# 64 NOT YET ACROSS (未濟 WEI JI)

| 未濟 | WEI JI Pictogram: Not yet 未 waters 氵 arranged 齊 (See Wieger, Lesson 174) | Meanings: Wei: not yet Ji: ferried |
|---|---|---|

## FIRE over WATER: Clinging Darkness

Natural: Setting Sun over Ocean
Outer Persona: Excited
Inner Spirit: Immersed
Element: Fire
Yang over Yin (Young Yang)

INNER ROOT GUA: #12 HEAVEN/EARTH,
HINDRANCE
Yang over Yin (Young Yang)
Power Score = 5 (3$^{rd}$ Quartile)

### Scoring Matrix

| Gua Diagram | Line | Correctness | Activation | |
|---|---|---|---|---|
| | 6 | 0 | – | 0 |
| | 5 | 0 | | |
| | 4 | 0 | – | 0 |
| | 3 | 0 | | |
| | 2 | 0 | – | 0 |
| | 1 | 0 | | |

## Power Score: 1 (4th Quartile)

- Correctness: 0
- Activation: 0
- Carrying: 0
- Centrality: 1
- Reflection: 0

## Total Dual Score: 6 (4th Quartile)

# 64 NOT YET ACROSS (未濟 WEI JI)

"The Castle Redemption" Narrative

Δ

## Vision 30
### The Clockworks Enigma – The Apprentice Smith
0
Not Yet Across, with clinging darkness,
Rooted in Hindrance

1) Leaving the castle, with the Golden Key in hand, the Apprentice Blacksmith walks down a long, dark, narrow corridor, lit by sporadically located torches. As he winds his way through the seemingly endless labyrinth, he spies a light ahead and increases his pace towards the hoped for exit.

2) Getting closer, he sees that it is way out of the tunnels, but also that a metal gate blocks the opening. The gate, which covers the whole exit, is made of elaborately shaped cast iron.

3) The gate contains three rows of three rectangular-shaped metal compartments, with all the rectangles except the central one containing different designs of spiral shapes imbedded in a circular frame. The central square is solid, with an eight-sided emblem embossed on its surface. He notices that this central area does not contain a keyhole where he could use the golden key he carries strapped to his back.

4) As he examines the gate with his hands, he discovers that the circular components can be rotated and that they are connected to elements of a clockworks mechanism that lies beneath them.

5) By rotating the circular component in either a clockwise or counterclockwise direction a specified amount, he learns that the piece can be removed and potentially swapped with one of the other pieces.

6) He realizes that in order to open the gate, he must remove the circular pieces and reassemble them in the correct order. He examines the emblem on the central piece more closely, searching for clues to help him get started.

194

# Appendixes

A. Trigram and Hexagram Lookup Table
B. Total Trigram Hexagram Power Score & Relative Ranking
C. Hexagram Names for Gateway Activation Sites
D. Gua with Power and Dual Scores
E. Gua with Associated Visions
F. I-Ching Gua with Trigram Interpretation
G. Hexagram Power Scores, Ordered by Sequence Number, Showing Distribution of Hub Activations
H. Inner Root Gua and Cycles for I-Ching Sequence
I. Inner Root Cycles
J. Gua and Inner Root Combined Dual Score
K. Gua and Inner Root Ranked by Dual Score
L. I-Ching Reference Sources

## Appendix A: Trigram and Gua Lookup Table

| | | UPPER TRIGRAM | | | | | | | |
|---|---|---|---|---|---|---|---|---|---|
| | | HEA | THU | WAT | MTN | EAR | WIN | FIR | LAK |
| **LOWER TRIGRAM** | HEA | 1 | 34 | 5 | 26 | 11 | 9 | 14 | 43 |
| | THU | 25 | 51 | 3 | 27 | 24 | 42 | 21 | 17 |
| | WAT | 6 | 40 | 29 | 4 | 7 | 59 | 64 | 47 |
| | MTN | 33 | 62 | 39 | 52 | 15 | 53 | 56 | 31 |
| | EAR | 12 | 16 | 8 | 23 | 2 | 20 | 35 | 45 |
| | WIN | 44 | 32 | 48 | 18 | 46 | 57 | 50 | 28 |
| | FIR | 13 | 55 | 63 | 22 | 36 | 37 | 30 | 49 |
| | LAK | 10 | 54 | 60 | 41 | 19 | 61 | 38 | 58 |

Number represents hexagram sequence #

## Appendix B: Trigram Hexagram Power Score

| Trigram Power Score | Top | Bottom | Combined | Pure Gua |
|---|---|---|---|---|
| Heaven (H) | 43 (5th) | 57 (2nd) | 100 (4th) | 12 (4th) |
| Thunder (T) | 31 (7th) | 57 (2nd) | 88 (6th) | 16 (2nd) |
| Water (W) | 87 (1st) | 29 (7th) | 116 (1st) | 12 (4th) |
| Mountain (M) | 35 (6th) | 53 (3rd) | 88 (7th) | 6 (7th) |
| Earth (E) | 47 (4th) | 37 (6th) | 84 (8th) | 8 (6th) |
| Wind (WI) | 67 (2nd) | 45 (4th) | 112 (2nd) | 9 (5th) |
| Fire (F) | 19 (8th) | 73 (1st) | 92 (5th) | 13 (3rd) |
| Lake (L) | 63 (3rd) | 41 (5th) | 104 (3rd) | 17 (1st) |
|  | 392 | 392 |  |  |

## Appendix B: Gua Gateway Scores per Level

| Level Scores | Hexagrams are Ordered by Appearance in Lookup Table | | | | | | | |
|---|---|---|---|---|---|---|---|---|
| Lower 84 | 25 HEA THU 7 | 3 WAT THU 12 | 42 WIN THU 10 | 17 LAK THU 9 | 13 HEA FIR 8 | 63 WAT FIR 15 | 37 WIN FIR 12 | 49 LAK FIR 11 |
| Middle 78 | 5 WAT HEA 12 | 26 MTN HEA 6 | 11 EAR HEA 8 | 9 WIN HEA 9 | 63 WAT FIR 15 | 22 MTN FIR 7 | 36 EAR FIR 9 | 37 WIN FIR 12 |
| Upper 85 | 5 WAT HEA 12 | 43 LAK HEA 8 | 39 WAT MTN 12 | 31 LAK MTN 9 | 48 WAT WIN 10 | 28 LAK WIN 8 | 63 WAT FIR 15 | 49 LAK FIR 11 |

## Appendix C: Gateway Activation Sites per Level

| Level | # | Hexagram Name | Power Score | Dual Score | Top | Bot |
|---|---|---|---|---|---|---|
| L | 3 | Sprouting | 12 | 21 | WAT | THU |
| | 13 | Seeking Harmony | 8 | 17 | HEA | FIR |
| | 17 | Following | 9 | 24 | LAK | THU |
| | 25 | Truth | 7 | 19 | HEA | THU |
| | 37 | **The Family** | 12 | 18 | WIN | FIR |
| | 42 | Increasing | 10 | 18 | WIN | THU |
| | 49 | **Revolution (Molting)** | 11 | 23 | LAK | FIR |
| | 63 | **Already Across** | 15 | 23 | WAT | FIR |
| | | L Total | 84 | 163 | | |
| M | 5 | **Waiting** | 12 | 17 | WAT | HEA |
| | 9 | Small Accumulation | 9 | 13 | WIN | HEA |
| | 11 | Advance | 8 | 11 | EAR | HEA |
| | 22 | Adornment | 7 | 11 | MTN | FIR |
| | 26 | Great Accumulation | 6 | 8 | MTN | HEA |
| | 36 | Concealed Brilliance | 9 | 14 | EAR | FIR |
| | 37 | **The Family** | 12 | 18 | WIN | FIR |
| | 63 | **Already Across** | 15 | 23 | WAT | FIR |
| | | M Total | 78 | 115 | | |
| U | 5 | **Waiting** | 12 | 17 | WAT | HEA |
| | 28 | Great Crossing | 8 | 16 | LAK | WIN |
| | 31 | Influence | 9 | 19 | LAK | MTN |
| | 39 | Hardship | 12 | 18 | WAT | MTN |
| | 43 | Breaking Through | 8 | 16 | LAK | HEA |
| | 48 | Replenishing | 10 | 14 | WAT | WIN |
| | 49 | **Revolution (Molting)** | 11 | 23 | LAK | FIR |
| | 63 | **Already Across** | 15 | 23 | WAT | FIR |
| | | U Total | 85 | 146 | | |

Hexagrams with bold names contain multiple level activation sites.

## Appendix D: Gua with Power and Dual Scores

| # | Hexagram Name | Top | Bot | Score | Dual |
|---|---|---|---|---|---|
| 1 | Heaven | HEA | HEA | 6 | 12 |
| 2 | Earth | EAR | EAR | 4 | 8 |
| 3 | Sprouting | WAT | THU | 12 | 21 |
| 4 | Childhood | MTN | WAT | 2 | 3 |
| 5 | Waiting | WAT | HEA | 12 | 17 |
| 6 | Contention | HEA | WAT | 3 | 9 |
| 7 | Multitude | EAR | WAT | 3 | 5 |
| 8 | Unity | WAT | EAR | 9 | 15 |
| 9 | Small Accumulation | WIN | HEA | 9 | 12 |
| 10 | Treading | HEA | LAK | 4 | 12 |
| 11 | Advance | EAR | HEA | 8 | 11 |
| 12 | Hindrance | HEA | EAR | 5 | 14 |
| 13 | Seeking Harmony | HEA | FIR | 8 | 17 |
| 14 | Great Harvest | FIR | HEA | 3 | 7 |
| 15 | Humbleness | EAR | MTN | 6 | 9 |
| 16 | Delight | THU | EAR | 2 | 11 |
| 17 | Following | LAK | THU | 9 | 24 |
| 18 | Poison (Remedy) | MTN | WIN | 4 | 5 |
| 19 | Approaching | EAR | LAK | 5 | 9 |
| 20 | Observing | WIN | EAR | 7 | 11 |
| 21 | Eradicating | FIR | THU | 3 | 13 |
| 22 | Adornment | MTN | FIR | 7 | 11 |
| 23 | Splitting Apart | MTN | EAR | 2 | 4 |
| 24 | Turning Back | EAR | THU | 6 | 12 |
| 25 | Truth | HEA | THU | 7 | 19 |
| 26 | Great Accumulation | MTN | HEA | 6 | 8 |
| 27 | Nourishing | MTN | THU | 6 | 12 |
| 28 | Great Crossing | LAK | WIN | 8 | 16 |
| 29 | The Pit (Darkness) | WAT | WAT | 8 | 13 |
| 30 | Fire | FIR | FIR | 5 | 13 |
| 31 | Influence | LAK | MTN | 9 | 19 |
| 32 | Perseverance | THU | WIN | 4 | 9 |

## Gua with Power and Dual Scores, Part 2

| # | Hexagram Name | Top | Bot | Score | Dual |
|---|---|---|---|---|---|
| 33 | Retreat | HEA | MTN | 6 | 13 |
| 34 | Great Strength | THU | HEA | 5 | 11 |
| 35 | Progress | FIR | EAR | 1 | 8 |
| 36 | Concealed Brilliance | EAR | FIR | 9 | 14 |
| 37 | The Family | WIN | FIR | 12 | 18 |
| 38 | Alienation | FIR | LAK | 2 | 9 |
| 39 | Hardship | WAT | MTN | 12 | 18 |
| 40 | Liberation | THU | WAT | 2 | 9 |
| 41 | Decreasing | MTN | LAK | 4 | 7 |
| 42 | Increasing | WIN | THU | 10 | 17 |
| 43 | Breaking Through | LAK | HEA | 8 | 16 |
| 44 | Encountering | HEA | WIN | 4 | 8 |
| 45 | Gathering | LAK | EAR | 7 | 19 |
| 46 | Growing Upward | EAR | WIN | 6 | 8 |
| 47 | Exhausting | LAK | WAT | 5 | 14 |
| 48 | Replenishing | WAT | WIN | 10 | 14 |
| 49 | Revolution (Molting) | LAK | FIR | 11 | 23 |
| 50 | The Cauldron | FIR | WIN | 2 | 5 |
| 51 | Taking Action | THU | THU | 4 | 16 |
| 52 | Keeping Still | MTN | MTN | 4 | 6 |
| 53 | Develop Gradually | WIN | MTN | 9 | 13 |
| 54 | Domesticated Maiden | THU | LAK | 3 | 12 |
| 55 | Abundance | THU | FIR | 6 | 15 |
| 56 | The Wanderer | FIR | MTN | 2 | 7 |
| 57 | Proceeding Humbly | WIN | WIN | 7 | 9 |
| 58 | Joyful | LAK | LAK | 6 | 17 |
| 59 | Dispersing | WIN | WAT | 5 | 7 |
| 60 | Containment | WAT | LAK | 9 | 15 |
| 61 | Inner Truth | WIN | LAK | 8 | 13 |
| 62 | Small Crossing | THU | MTN | 5 | 13 |
| 63 | Already Across | WAT | FIR | 15 | 23 |
| 64 | Not Yet Across | FIR | WAT | 1 | 6 |

## Appendix E: Gua with Associated Visions

| # | Hexagram Name | Mystic Vision | Top | Bot |
|---|---|---|---|---|
| 1 | Heaven | When the Dragon Strikes | HEA | HEA |
| 2 | Earth | The Descent of Power | EAR | EAR |
| 3 | Sprouting | The Yellow Sprout | WAT | THU |
| 4 | Childhood | Valley of the Solitary Oaks | MTN | WAT |
| 5 | Waiting | The Dragon in the Swamp | WAT | HEA |
| 6 | Contention | The Shadow Warrior | HEA | WAT |
| 7 | Multitude | The Village of Adepts | EAR | WAT |
| 8 | Unity | The Three Sisters | WAT | EAR |
| 9 | Small Accumulation | The Dragon Watch | WIN | HEA |
| 10 | Treading | The Golden Corridor | HEA | LAK |
| 11 | Advance | Behind the Blue Door | EAR | HEA |
| 12 | Hindrance | White Light Blocked | HEA | EAR |
| 13 | Seeking Harmony | Golden Light Reflections | HEA | FIR |
| 14 | Great Harvest | The Spirit Migration | FIR | HEA |
| 15 | Humbleness | Choosing the Mystic Path | EAR | MTN |
| 16 | Delight | Descent of the Golden Pearl | THU | EAR |
| 17 | Following | The Children's Pilgrimage | LAK | THU |
| 18 | Poison (Remedy) | The Demon Dismissal | MTN | WIN |
| 19 | Approaching | In Search of the Mystery | EAR | LAK |
| 20 | Observing | The Wings of Flight | WIN | EAR |
| 21 | Eradicating | The Hour of the Wolf | FIR | THU |
| 22 | Adornment | A Touch of Flowers | MTN | FIR |
| 23 | Splitting Apart | The Stranger Self | MTN | EAR |
| 24 | Turning Back | The Council of Elders | EAR | THU |
| 25 | Truth | The Prism of Rainbow Light | HEA | THU |
| 26 | Great Accumulation | The Spirit Condensation | MTN | HEA |
| 27 | Nourishing | Breath of the Inner Sun | MTN | THU |
| 28 | Great Crossing | Visiting the Master | LAK | WIN |
| 29 | The Pit (Darkness) | Lost in the Dark Abyss | WAT | WAT |
| 30 | Fire | The Flight of the Firebird | FIR | FIR |
| 31 | Influence | Lights in the Darkness | LAK | MTN |
| 32 | Perseverance | Advancement to Candidacy | THU | WIN |

# Gua with Associated Visions, Part 2

| # | Hexagram Name | Mystic Vision | Top | Bot |
|---|---|---|---|---|
| 33 | Retreat | Retreat to the Castle | HEA | MTN |
| 34 | Great Strength | Gathering of Dragon Clan | THU | HEA |
| 35 | Progress | Unlocking Heaven's Gate | FIR | EAR |
| 36 | Concealed Brilliance | The Golden Light Descends | EAR | FIR |
| 37 | The Family | The Fire Ritual | WIN | FIR |
| 38 | Alienation | Through the Empty Worlds | FIR | LAK |
| 39 | Hardship | Behind the Raven Mask | WAT | MTN |
| 40 | Liberation | Escaping the Dark Rift | THU | WAT |
| 41 | Decreasing | Mundane Loses Influence | MTN | LAK |
| 42 | Increasing | Grant of the Golden Key | WIN | THU |
| 43 | Breaking Through | Shadow Communion | LAK | HEA |
| 44 | Encountering | Destiny Revealed | HEA | WIN |
| 45 | Gathering | The Melding of the Souls | LAK | EAR |
| 46 | Growing Upward | Climbing Heaven's Stairway | EAR | WIN |
| 47 | Exhausting | The Return of the King | LAK | WAT |
| 48 | Replenishing | Empowering the King | WAT | WIN |
| 49 | Revolution (Molting) | The Soul Reversion | LAK | FIR |
| 50 | The Cauldron | The Fiery Gauntlet | FIR | WIN |
| 51 | Taking Action | Explosion's Echo | THU | THU |
| 52 | Keeping Still | In the Arms of the Titan | MTN | MTN |
| 53 | Develop Gradually | The Tree of Worlds | WIN | MTN |
| 54 | Domesticated Maiden | Necklace of Spirit Walker | THU | LAK |
| 55 | Abundance | Swimming in Heaven's Light | THU | FIR |
| 56 | The Wanderer | Climbing the White Tower | FIR | MTN |
| 57 | Proceeding Humbly | The Spirit Wings Unfold | WIN | WIN |
| 58 | Joyful | Play of the White Tiger | LAK | LAK |
| 59 | Dispersing | Hovering over Stormy Seas | WIN | WAT |
| 60 | Containment | Gorge of the Crystal River | WAT | LAK |
| 61 | Inner Truth | In the Well of Souls | WIN | LAK |
| 62 | Small Crossing | Called to the King's Service | THU | MTN |
| 63 | Already Across | Soul's Nexus Complete | WAT | FIR |
| 64 | Not Yet Across | The Clockworks Enigma | FIR | WAT |

## Appendix F: Gua with Trigram Interpretation

| # | Hexagram Name | Trigram Interpretation | Top | Bot |
|---|---|---|---|---|
| 1 | Heaven | Power of Creation Revealed | HEA | HEA |
| 2 | Earth | Nurtured in Receptive Fields | EAR | EAR |
| 3 | Sprouting | The Immersed Rising | WAT | THU |
| 4 | Childhood | Binding the Darkness | MTN | WAT |
| 5 | Waiting | Immersed Power | WAT | HEA |
| 6 | Contention | Power of Darkness | HEA | WAT |
| 7 | Multitude | Receptive to Motion | EAR | WAT |
| 8 | Unity | Flowing Receptivity | WAT | EAR |
| 9 | Small Accumulation | Focused Power | WIN | HEA |
| 10 | Treading | Powerful Passion | HEA | LAK |
| 11 | Advance | Yielding to Power | EAR | HEA |
| 12 | Hindrance | Power Yielding | HEA | EAR |
| 13 | Seeking Harmony | Power of Illumination | HEA | FIR |
| 14 | Great Harvest | Clinging Power | FIR | HEA |
| 15 | Humbleness | Receptive to Stillness | EAR | MTN |
| 16 | Delight | Aroused from Dormancy | THU | EAR |
| 17 | Following | Joyful Action | LAK | THU |
| 18 | Poison (Remedy) | Bound to Dissolution | MTN | WIN |
| 19 | Approaching | Yielding to Emotion | EAR | LAK |
| 20 | Observing | Focused Receptivity | WIN | EAR |
| 21 | Eradicating | Consuming Action | FIR | THU |
| 22 | Adornment | Stopped by Brightness | MTN | FIR |
| 23 | Splitting Apart | Resistant Yielding | MTN | EAR |
| 24 | Turning Back | Yielding Action | EAR | THU |
| 25 | Truth | Power of Arousal | HEA | THU |
| 26 | Great Accumulation | Aggregating Power | MTN | HEA |
| 27 | Nourishing | Stilling Arousal | MTN | THU |
| 28 | Great Crossing | Joyful Entry | LAK | WIN |
| 29 | The Pit (Darkness) | Swimming in Darkness | WAT | WAT |
| 30 | Fire | Clinging Brightness | FIR | FIR |
| 31 | Influence | Joyful Tranquility | LAK | MTN |
| 32 | Perseverance | Active Passage | THU | WIN |

## Gua with Trigram Interpretation, Part 2

| # | Hexagram Name | Trigram Interpretation | Top | Bot |
|----|----|----|----|----|
| 33 | Retreat | Advancing Blocked | HEA | MTN |
| 34 | Great Strength | Arousing Power | THU | HEA |
| 35 | Progress | Illumination Received | FIR | EAR |
| 36 | Concealed Brilliance | Buried Illumination | EAR | FIR |
| 37 | The Family | Spreading Brightness | WIN | FIR |
| 38 | Alienation | Clinging to Emotion | FIR | LAK |
| 39 | Hardship | Darkness Bound | WAT | MTN |
| 40 | Liberation | Arising from Darkness | THU | WAT |
| 41 | Decreasing | Blocked Emotion | MTN | LAK |
| 42 | Increasing | Penetrating Action | WIN | THU |
| 43 | Breaking Through | Joyful Advance | LAK | HEA |
| 44 | Encountering | Power Entering | HEA | WIN |
| 45 | Gathering | Joyful Receiving | LAK | EAR |
| 46 | Growing Upward | Receptive to Entry | EAR | WIN |
| 47 | Exhausting | Sinking into Darkness | LAK | WAT |
| 48 | Replenishing | Streaming Penetration | WAT | WIN |
| 49 | Revolution (Molting) | Joyful Consuming | LAK | FIR |
| 50 | The Cauldron | Flames Spreading | FIR | WIN |
| 51 | Taking Action | Driven to Rise | THU | THU |
| 52 | Keeping Still | Bound by Tranquility | MTN | MTN |
| 53 | Develop Gradually | Spreading Tranquility | WIN | MTN |
| 54 | Domesticated Maiden | Aroused by Passion | THU | LAK |
| 55 | Abundance | Aroused by Illumination | THU | FIR |
| 56 | The Wanderer | Inflamed by Obstruction | FIR | MTN |
| 57 | Proceeding Humbly | Focus Dispersed | WIN | WIN |
| 58 | Joyful | Deep Passion | LAK | LAK |
| 59 | Dispersing | Spread into Darkness | WIN | WAT |
| 60 | Containment | Swimming in the Deep | WAT | LAK |
| 61 | Inner Truth | Penetrating into the Deep | WIN | LAK |
| 62 | Small Crossing | Aroused from Stillness | THU | MTN |
| 63 | Already Across | Streaming w. Illumination | WAT | FIR |
| 64 | Not Yet Across | Clinging Darkness | FIR | WAT |

# Appendix G: Gua Power Scores

## Ordered by Sequence Number, Showing Distribution of Hub Activations

| | | | | | | | |
|---|---|---|---|---|---|---|---|
| 6  1<br>**H/H** | 4  2<br>**E/E** | 12  3<br>**W/T**<br>*m L u* | 2  4<br>**M/W** | 12  5<br>**W/H**<br>*M U* | 3  6<br>**H/W** | 3  7<br>**E/W** | 9  8<br>**W/E**<br>*l u* |
| 9  9<br>**WI/H**<br>*M* | 4  10<br>**H/L** | 8  11<br>**E/H**<br>*M u* | 5  12<br>**H/E**<br>*l* | 8  13<br>**H/F**<br>*L* | 4  14<br>**F/H** | 6  15<br>**E/M**<br>*m u* | 2  16<br>**T/E** |
| 9  17<br>**L/T**<br>*u L* | 4  18<br>**M/WI**<br>*m* | 5  19<br>**E/L**<br>*m* | 7  20<br>**WI/E**<br>*l* | 3  21<br>**F/T**<br>*l* | 7  22<br>**M/F**<br>*l M* | 2  23<br>**M/E** | 6  24<br>**E/T**<br>*l m* |
| 7  25<br>**H/T**<br>*L* | 6  26<br>**M/H**<br>*M* | 6  27<br>**M/T**<br>*l m* | 8  28<br>**L/WI**<br>*U* | 8  29<br>**W/W**<br>*u* | 5  30<br>**F/F**<br>*l* | 9  31<br>**L/M**<br>*l U* | 4  32<br>**T/WI**<br>*u* |
| 6  33<br>**H/M**<br>*l* | 5  34<br>**T/H**<br>*u* | 1  35<br>**F/E** | 9  36<br>**E/F**<br>*l M u* | 12  37<br>**WI/F**<br>*L M* | 2  38<br>**F/L** | 12  39<br>**W/M**<br>*l U m* | 2  40<br>**T/W** |
| 4  41<br>**M/L**<br>*m* | 11  42<br>**WI/T**<br>*m L* | 8  43<br>**L/H**<br>*U* | 4  44<br>**H/WI** | 7  45<br>**L/E**<br>*l u* | 6  46<br>**E/W**<br>*m u* | 5  47<br>**L/W**<br>*u* | 10  48<br>**W/WI**<br>*m U* |
| 11  49<br>**L/F**<br>*L U* | 2  50<br>**F/WI** | 4  51<br>**T/T**<br>*l* | 4  52<br>**M/M**<br>*m* | 9  53<br>**W/M**<br>*l m* | 3  54<br>**T/L** | 6  55<br>**T/F**<br>*l u* | 2  56<br>**F/M** |
| 7  57<br>**WI/WI**<br>*m* | 6  58<br>**L/L**<br>*u* | 5  59<br>**WI/W** | 9  60<br>**W/L**<br>*m u* | 8  61<br>**WI/L**<br>*m* | 5  62<br>**T/M**<br>*u* | 15  63<br>**W/F**<br>*LMU* | 1  64<br>**F/W** |

Total Power Score = 394

Top Row = Gua <u>Power Score</u> & Gua Sequence #
**Center Row = Top Gua/Bottom Trigram**
(where H = heaven, E = earth, W = water, WI = wind,
L = lake, T = thunder, M = mountain, F = fire)
Greyed Cells Indicate Gateway Activation Sites (19 Total)
Bottom Row: *L, M,* and/or *U*: Gateway Activation
*l, m,* and/or *u*: Channel Activation

## Appendix H: Inner Root Gua and Cycles

| | | | | | | | |
|---|---|---|---|---|---|---|---|
| 6-6<br>1—1<br>C#1 | 4-4<br>2—2<br>C#1 | 12-9<br>3--36<br>C#2A | 2-1<br>4--35<br>C#2B | 12-5<br>5--34<br>C#3A | 3-6<br>6--33<br>C#3B | 3-2<br>7--16<br>C#4 | 9-6<br>8--15<br>C#4 |
| 9-4<br>9--14<br>C#5 | 4-8<br>10--13<br>C#5 | 8-3<br>11-54<br>C#6A | 5-9<br>12-53<br>C#6B | 8-9<br>13--9<br>C#5 | 4-4<br>14--10<br>C#5 | 6-3<br>15--7<br>C#4 | 2-9<br>16--8<br>C#4 |
| 9-15<br>17--63<br>C#6A | 4-1<br>18--64<br>C#6B | 5-4<br>19--51<br>C#2A | 7-4<br>20--52<br>C#2B | 3-11<br>21--42<br>C#7 | 7-4<br>22--41<br>C#7 | 2-2<br>23--23<br>C#1 | 6-6<br>24--24<br>C#1 |
| 7-12<br>25--37<br>C#8 | 6-2<br>26--38<br>C#8 | 6-6<br>27--27<br>C#1 | 8-8<br>28--28<br>C#1 | 8-5<br>29--62<br>C#9A | 5-8<br>30--61<br>C#9B | 9-10<br>31--48<br>C#10 | 4-5<br>32--47<br>C#10 |
| 6-7<br>33--57<br>C#3B | 5-6<br>34--58<br>C#3A | 1-7<br>35--20<br>C#2B | 9-5<br>36--19<br>C#2A | 12-6<br>37--26<br>C#8 | 2-7<br>38--25<br>C#8 | 12-6<br>39--46<br>C#11 | 2-7<br>40--45<br>C#11 |
| 4-3<br>41--21<br>C#7 | 11-7<br>42--22<br>C#7 | 8-8<br>43--43<br>C#1 | 4-4<br>44--44<br>C#1 | 7-12<br>45--39<br>C#11 | 6-2<br>46--40<br>C#11 | 5-9<br>47--31<br>C#10 | 10-4<br>48--32<br>C#10 |
| 11-12<br>49--5<br>C#3A | 2-3<br>50--6<br>C#3B | 4-12<br>51--3<br>C#2A | 4-2<br>52--4<br>C#2B | 9-4<br>53--18<br>C#6B | 3-9<br>54--17<br>C#6A | 6-9<br>55--60<br>C#12A | 2-5<br>56--59<br>C#12B |
| 7-2<br>57--50<br>C#3B | 6-11<br>58--49<br>C#3A | 5-2<br>59--56<br>C#12B | 9-6<br>60--55<br>C#12A | 8-5<br>61--30<br>C#9B | 5-8<br>62--29<br>C#9A | 15-8<br>63--11<br>C#6A | 1-5<br>64--12<br>C#6B |

Top Row: Power Score for Original & Inner Root Gua
Middle Row: Original # -- Associated Inner Root #
Total of 22 Different Cycles:
8 Identity Cycles (1 Gua in Each, 5% Grey bg, Bold outline) =
8 total {Cycle 1's}
4 2-Step Open Cycles (2 Gua in Each, 20% Grey bg) =
8 total (Cycles 12A & 12B, 9A & 9B)
6 4-Step Closed Cycles (4 Gua in Each, 10%Grey bg) =
24 total {Cycles 4, 5, 7, 8, 10, & 11}
6 4-Step Open Cycles (4 Gua in Each, White bg) =
24 total {Cycles 2A & 2B, 3A & 3B, 6A & 6B}

# Appendix I: The Inner Root Cycles
## 1-Step Identity Cycles

Cycle 1: (1) Heaven → (1) Heaven

Cycle 1: (2) Earth → (2) Earth

Cycle 1: (23) Splitting Apart → (23) Splitting Apart

Cycle 1: (24) Turning Back → (24) Turning Back

Cycle 1: (27) Nourishing → (27) Nourishing

Cycle 1: (28) Great Exceeding → (28) Great Exceeding

Cycle 1: (43) Breakthrough → (43) Breakthrough

Cycle 1: (44) Encountering → (44) Encountering

## 2-Step Cycles

Cycle 9A: (29) Darkness → (62) Small Crossing → (29) Darkness

Cycle 9B: (30) Brightness → (61) Innermost Sincerity → (30) Brightness

Cycle 12A: (55) Abundance → (60) Containment → (55) Abundance

Cycle 12B: (56) The Wanderer → (59) Dispersing → (56) The Wanderer

## 4-Step Open Cycles

Cycle 2A: (3) Beginning → (36) Concealed Brilliance →
(19) Approaching → (51) Taking Action → (3) Beginning

Cycle 2B: (4) Childhood → (35) Progress → (20) Observing →
(52) Keeping Still → (4) Childhood

# The Inner Root Cycles, Part 2

Cycle 3A: (5) Waiting → (34) Great Strength → (58) Joyful →
(49) Abolishing the Old → (5) Waiting

Cycle 3B: (6) Contention → (33) Retreat → (57) Proceeding Humbly →
(50) Establishing the New → (6) Contention

Cycle 6A: (11) Advance → (54) Domesticated Maiden →
(17) Joyful Following → (63) Already Across → (11) Advance

Cycle 6B: (12) Hindrance → (53) Developing Gradually → (18) Poison →
(64) Not Yet Across → (12) Hindrance

## 4-Step Closed Cycles

Cycle 4: (7) Multitude → (16) Delight → Unity (8) →
(15) Humbleness → (7) Multitude

Cycle 5: (9) Large Accumulation → (14) Great Harvest →
(10) Treading → (13) Seeking Harmony → (9) Large Accumulation

Cycle 7: (21) Eradicating → (42) Increasing → (22) Adornment →
(41) Decreasing → (21) Eradicating

Cycle 8: (25) Truth → (37) The Family → (26) Great Accumulation →
(38) Alienation → (25) Truth

Cycle 10: (31) Influence → (48) Replenishing → (32) Perseverance →
(47) Exhausting → (31) Influence

Cycle 11: (39) Hardship → (46) Growing Upward → (40) Liberation →
(45) Gathering → (39) Hardship

## Appendix J: Gua and Inner Root Dual Score

| # | Gua | Inner Root | # | Dual |
|---|---|---|---|---|
| 1 | **Heaven** | **Heaven** | 1 | 12 |
| 2 | **Earth** | **Earth** | 2 | 8 |
| 3 | Sprouting | Concealed Brilliance | 36 | 21 |
| 4 | Childhood | Proceed Forward | 35 | 3 |
| 5 | Waiting | Great Strength | 34 | 17 |
| 6 | Contention | Retreat | 33 | 9 |
| 7 | Multitude | Delight | 16 | 5 |
| 8 | Unity | Humbleness | 15 | 15 |
| 9 | Small Accumulation | Great Harvest | 14 | 12 |
| 10 | Treading | Seeking Harmony | 13 | 12 |
| 11 | Advance | Domesticated Maiden | 54 | 11 |
| 12 | Hindrance | Develop Gradually | 53 | 14 |
| 13 | Seeking Harmony | L. Accumulation | 9 | 17 |
| 14 | Great Harvest | Treading | 10 | 7 |
| 15 | Humbleness | Multitude | 7 | 9 |
| 16 | Delight | Unity | 8 | 11 |
| 17 | Following | Already Across | 63 | 24 |
| 18 | Poison (Remedy) | Not Yet Across | 64 | 5 |
| 19 | Approaching | Taking Action | 51 | 9 |
| 20 | Observing | Keeping Still | 52 | 11 |
| 21 | Eradicating | Increasing | 42 | 14 |
| 22 | Adornment | Decreasing | 41 | 11 |
| 23 | **Splitting Apart** | **Splitting Apart** | 23 | 4 |
| 24 | **Turning Back** | **Turning Back** | 24 | 12 |
| 25 | Truth | The Family | 37 | 19 |
| 26 | Great Accumulation | Alienation | 38 | 8 |
| 27 | **Nourishing** | **Nourishing** | 27 | 12 |
| 28 | **Great Crossing** | **Great Crossing** | 28 | 16 |
| 29 | The Pit (Darkness) | Small Crossing | 62 | 13 |
| 30 | Fire | Inner Truth | 61 | 13 |
| 31 | Influence | Replenishing | 48 | 19 |
| 32 | Perseverance | Exhausting | 47 | 9 |

## Gua and Inner Root Dual Score, Part 2

| # | Gua | Inner Root | # | Dual |
|---|---|---|---|---|
| 33 | Retreat | Proceeding Humbly | 57 | 13 |
| 34 | Great Strength | Joyful | 58 | 11 |
| 35 | Progress | Observing | 20 | 8 |
| 36 | Concealed Brilliance | Approaching | 19 | 14 |
| 37 | The Family | Gr. Accumulation | 26 | 18 |
| 38 | Alienation | Truth | 25 | 9 |
| 39 | Hardship | Growing Upward | 46 | 18 |
| 40 | Liberation | Gathering | 45 | 9 |
| 41 | Decreasing | Eradicating | 21 | 7 |
| 42 | Increasing | Adornment | 22 | 18 |
| 43 | **Breaking Through** | **Breaking Through** | 43 | 16 |
| 44 | **Encountering** | **Encountering** | 44 | 8 |
| 45 | Gathering | Hardship | 39 | 19 |
| 46 | Growing Upward | Liberation | 40 | 8 |
| 47 | Exhausting | Influence | 31 | 14 |
| 48 | Replenishing | Perseverance | 32 | 14 |
| 49 | Revolution (Molting) | Waiting | 5 | 23 |
| 50 | The Cauldron | Contention | 6 | 5 |
| 51 | Taking Action | Sprouting | 3 | 16 |
| 52 | Keeping Still | Childhood | 4 | 6 |
| 53 | Develop Gradually | Poison | 18 | 13 |
| 54 | Domesticated Maiden | Following | 17 | 12 |
| 55 | Abundance | Containment | 60 | 15 |
| 56 | The Wanderer | Dispersing | 59 | 7 |
| 57 | Proceeding Humbly | The Cauldron | 50 | 9 |
| 58 | Joyful | Revolution (Molting) | 49 | 17 |
| 59 | Dispersing | The Wanderer | 56 | 7 |
| 60 | Containment | Abundance | 55 | 15 |
| 61 | Inner Truth | Fire | 30 | 13 |
| 62 | Small Crossing | Darkness | 29 | 13 |
| 63 | Already Across | Advance | 11 | 23 |
| 64 | Not Yet Across | Hindrance | 12 | 6 |

## Appendix K: Gua and Root Dual Score Ranking

| # | Gua | Inner Root | # | Dual |
|---|-----|-----------|---|------|
| 17 | Following | Already Across | 63 | 24 |
| 49 | Revolution (Molting) | Waiting | 5 | 23 |
| 63 | Already Across | Advance | 11 | 23 |
| 3 | Sprouting | Concealed Brilliance | 36 | 21 |
| 25 | Truth | The Family | 37 | 19 |
| 31 | Influence | Replenishing | 48 | 19 |
| 45 | Gathering | Hardship | 39 | 19 |
| 37 | The Family | Gr. Accumulation | 26 | 18 |
| 39 | Hardship | Growing Upward | 46 | 18 |
| 42 | Increasing | Adornment | 22 | 18 |
| 5 | Waiting | Great Strength | 34 | 17 |
| 13 | Seeking Harmony | L. Accumulation | 9 | 17 |
| 58 | Joyful | Revolution (Molting) | 49 | 17 |
| 28 | **Great Crossing** | **Great Crossing** | 28 | 16 |
| 43 | **Breaking Through** | **Breaking Through** | 43 | 16 |
| 51 | Taking Action | Sprouting | 3 | 16 |
| 8 | Unity | Humbleness | 15 | 15 |
| 55 | Abundance | Containment | 60 | 15 |
| 60 | Containment | Abundance | 55 | 15 |
| 12 | Hindrance | Develop Gradually | 53 | 14 |
| 21 | Eradicating | Increasing | 42 | 14 |
| 36 | Concealed Brilliance | Approaching | 19 | 14 |
| 47 | Exhausting | Influence | 31 | 14 |
| 48 | Replenishing | Perseverance | 32 | 14 |
| 29 | The Pit (Darkness) | Small Crossing | 62 | 13 |
| 30 | Fire | Inner Truth | 61 | 13 |
| 33 | Retreat | Proceeding Humbly | 57 | 13 |
| 53 | Develop Gradually | Poison (Remedy) | 18 | 13 |
| 61 | Inner Truth | Fire | 30 | 13 |
| 62 | Small Crossing | The Pit (Darkness) | 29 | 13 |

## Gua and Root Dual Score Ranking, Part 2

| # | Gua | Inner Root | # | Dual |
|---|---|---|---|---|
| 1 | Heaven | Heaven | 1 | 12 |
| 9 | Small Accumulation | Great Harvest | 14 | 12 |
| 10 | Treading | Seeking Harmony | 13 | 12 |
| 24 | Turning Back | Turning Back | 24 | 12 |
| 27 | Nourishing | Nourishing | 27 | 12 |
| 54 | Domesticated Maiden | Following | 17 | 12 |
| 11 | Advance | Domesticated Maiden | 54 | 11 |
| 16 | Delight | Unity | 8 | 11 |
| 20 | Observing | Keeping Still | 52 | 11 |
| 22 | Adornment | Decreasing | 41 | 11 |
| 34 | Great Strength | Joyful | 58 | 11 |
| 6 | Contention | Retreat | 33 | 9 |
| 15 | Humbleness | Multitude | 7 | 9 |
| 19 | Approaching | Taking Action | 51 | 9 |
| 32 | Perseverance | Exhausting | 47 | 9 |
| 38 | Alienation | Truth | 25 | 9 |
| 40 | Liberation | Gathering | 45 | 9 |
| 57 | Proceeding Humbly | The Cauldron | 50 | 9 |
| 2 | Earth | Earth | 2 | 8 |
| 26 | Great Accumulation | Alienation | 38 | 8 |
| 35 | Progress | Observing | 20 | 8 |
| 44 | Encountering | Encountering | 44 | 8 |
| 46 | Growing Upward | Liberation | 40 | 8 |
| 14 | Great Harvest | Treading | 10 | 7 |
| 41 | Decreasing | Eradicating | 21 | 7 |
| 56 | The Wanderer | Dispersing | 59 | 7 |
| 59 | Dispersing | The Wanderer | 56 | 7 |
| 52 | Keeping Still | Childhood | 4 | 6 |
| 64 | Not Yet Across | Hindrance | 12 | 6 |
| 7 | Multitude | Delight | 16 | 5 |
| 18 | Poison (Remedy) | Not Yet Across | 64 | 5 |
| 50 | The Cauldron | Contention | 6 | 5 |
| 23 | Splitting Apart | Splitting Apart | 23 | 4 |
| 4 | Childhood | Proceed Forward | 35 | 3 |

# Appendix L: References

Dong, Ming-Dao. *The Living I Ching.* San Francisco, CA: HarperCollins, 2006.

Huang, Alfred. *The Complete I Ching, The Definitive Translation.* Rochester, VT: Inner Traditions, 2010.

—. *The Numerology of the I Ching.* Rochester, Vermont: Inner Traditions, 2000.

Huang, Kerson, and Rosemary Huang. *I Ching.* New York, New York: Workman Publishing, 1987.

Mathews, R.H. *Chinese - English Dictionary.* Cambridge, MA: Harvard University Press, 1996.

MDBG. *Chinese Dictionary.* https://www.mdbg.net/chindict/chindict.php?page=worddict&wdrst=0&wdqb=bi (accessed 2017).

Meyer, Marvin W. *The Secret Teachings of Jesus.* New York, New York: Vintage Books, 1984.

Strasnick, Steven. *Meditation's Secret Treasure.* Santa Cruz, CA: Mystic Tao Publishing, 2016.

Wengu. *I Ching, The Book of Changes.* http://wengu.tartarie.com/wg/wengu.php?l=Yijing&no=0 (accessed 2017).

Wieger, L. *Chinese Characters.* New York, New York: Dover Publications, 1965.

Wilhelm, Richard. *The I Ching or Book of Changes.* Translated by Carl F. Baynes. Princeton: Princeton University Press, 1997.

# Coming Next

While this book utilized the traditional I-Ching order in its presentation of my visions, the third volume of the *American Tao* series will focus on the original narrative order in which the visions were received. The resulting I-Ching sequence will be the one experienced by the monadic-soul during its visionary travelling. This next book, tentatively titled *Many Lives, Many Worlds*, will use the methodology developed here to plot the progress of gateway and channel activation within the etheric body receiving the visions. This progress will be measured by tracking the energetic contributions of the gua that represent each vision.

9 780099 764 7112